"WE ARE BECOMING AWARE NOW

. . . of the disease of affluence—greed, slavery to things, tyrannical technology, insidiously powerful advertising, shallow and immoral economy based solely on production growth, temptation to conspicuous consumption.

"And, at the same time, . . . we are seeing— sometimes to the point of callousness — the malnutrition, the broken homes, the idleness, the crime, the despair, and the anger which are so widespread both in the city ghetto and in the rural slum.

"At both extremes of the scale, human life becomes degraded and brutish. . . ."

"In this book, we shall try to see how we can live simply in relation to several of the major issues which seem to threaten the very foundations of human existence today."

—The Author

SIMPLE LIVING

•

EDWARD K. ZIEGLER

THE BRETHREN PRESS   •   ELGIN, ILLINOIS

SIMPLE LIVING

Published by Pyramid Publications for The Brethren Press

First printing October, 1974

ISBN: 0-87178-791-1

Library of Congress Catalog Card Number: 74-8716

Copyright © 1974 by The Brethren Press

Printed in the United States of America

THE BRETHREN PRESS
Elgin, Illinois 60120, U.S.A.

'Tis a gift to be simple, 'Tis a gift to be free,
'Tis a gift to come down where we ought to be.
And when we find ourselves in the place just right
'Twill be in the valley of love and delight.
When true simplicity is gained
To bow and to bend we shan't be ashamed.
To turn, turn will be our delight,
'Till by turning, turning we come round right.

SHAKER FOLKSONG

Acknowledgments and Permission

All possible care has been taken to make full acknowledgments for materials quoted. If any errors have accidentally occurred, they will be corrected with full apology in subsequent editions, provided notification is sent to the publisher.

From "Why We Live in Community" by Eberhard Arnold, used by permission of the Society of Brothers.

From a letter and mimeographed material from Julius Belser of the Reba Place Fellowship.

From *The Christian Ministry*. Used by permission of that journal.

From *Cultural Changes in the Church of the Brethren* by Frederick D. Dove. Copyright 1932. Used by permission of Frederick Dove, Jr.

Statement by Margaret Mead from *To Love or To Perish*, edited by J. Edward Carothers, Margaret Mead, Daniel J. McCracken, and Roger Shinn. Copyright 1972, Friendship Press, New York. Used by permission.

From *The New English Bible*. Copyright 1961, 1970 by The Delegates of the Oxford University Press and The Syndics of the Cambridge University Press. Reprinted by permission.

From *A Sand County Almanac with other essays on conversation from Round River*, by Aldo Leopold. Copyright 1949, 1953, 1966 by Oxford University Press, Inc. Reprinted by permission.

From *The Simple Life* by Vernard Eller. Copyright 1973 by Wm. B. Eerdmans Publishing Company. Used by permission.

From *Mennonite Attire Through Four Centuries* by Melvin Gingerich. The Pennsylvania German Society, 1970.

From *An Investigation of the Origin, Significance, and Demise of the Prescribed Dress Worn by Members of the Church of the Brethren*, by Esther Fern Rupel. Thesis submitted to the faculty of the Graduate School of the University of Minnesota for the Ph.D. Degree, 1971 (Unpublished).

CONTENTS

PREFACE

How can we live a simple, uncluttered, serene life in the midst of our modern, urban, sophisticated, technological society? In an attempt to answer this question we will look at the concept and practice of the simple life as lived and taught by those known as the Church of the Brethren. They have historically sought to live simply and continue to see simplicity as a desirable and attainable contemporary life-style.

We will also consider whether we can, without withdrawing from society, regain many of the values found in the life of the earlier Brethren. We will seek to establish that a Christian life-style can not only exist in such a world as ours, but that it should.

As we try to discover what life-styles are relevant and workable today, we should remember that the historical Brethren life-styles were not a retreat from society. They were a response to the world of that day. This group of dedicated followers of Christ tried to live in its world as a colony of the Kingdom of God, at peace with its neighbors and strongly knit into congregations which were communities of faith. As such, these Brethren were always in tension with the evolving society around them.

In this book we will try to picture what true "simple living" might be in this time in which we are called to live and to give life. Will Durant says, "The Oriental is rich in the simplicity of his needs."

Kierkegaard defined purity of heart as "to will one thing." We will think of the simple life, too, as life lived by the standards and priorities of Jesus Christ, as we can discover them in the New Testament. We will see this life as lived in perfect harmony with the Christian doctrine of creation, in holy obedience to God, and in loving, sharing, compassionate relationship with our brothers and sisters in the whole human family.

Many years ago, Brethren social actionist Dan West, in correspondence with a Mennonite author, wrote his thoughts on simple living in these words:

"My conviction is that simplicity is related essentially to integrity, that the simple life is the integrated life with all of the essentials included, with all marginal values, 'accessories,' excluded. From this point of view, simplicity is possible on many levels and in many varied situations. There is a simple faith of persons who take the New Testament literally, not knowing the background. There's another simple faith achieved by great scholars who round the circle of learning with a humble heart. Someone observed that 'Perfect ignorance is calm. Perfect knowledge is calm. In between is the storm.' That is directly related to the idea of simplicity."

This quality of simple, uncluttered living is a golden mean between a rigid, joyless, life-denying asceticism on the one side, and an unbuttoned, selfish, life-denying hedonism on the other. And in this book we shall try to see how we can live simply, in joy and freedom, in relation to several of the major issues which seem to threaten the very foundations of human existence today.

—EDWARD K. ZIEGLER

INTRODUCTION

The growing concern of many Christians to find life-styles which conserve the good of earlier "simple living" is manifest in many aspects of our common life.

The worldwide growing sensitivity to the waste of wild creatures, the pollution of lakes, rivers, the oceans and the atmosphere, compels us to examine our personal and corporate life-styles, if we and our children are to have a habitable world. There is a flood of books, articles, and mass media presentations on ecology and conservation of the environment. It is becoming clear that no one on Earth can live a good and healthy life much longer unless we can all learn to exercise a better stewardship of the resources we have and can reverse the horrendous march of pollution and despoliation.

The protests against economic and racial injustice, war, affluence, and conventional standards of living have often taken bizarre and even destructive forms. The youth countercultures, the million runaway boys and girls in this country are a part of this vast and ominous protest. Often the background of all these symptoms is a hopeless and disgusted rejection of the mad, affluent materialism of our age.

The rising tide of disillusionment and cynicism over "big government" also reflects this concern. The scandals, the awesome power of the military industrial complex, the insensitivity to the needs of the poor, the aged, the sick, the minority groups,

have bred in thoughtful people a nostalgia for forms
of "purer" democracy. They hope for a time when
a concerned citizen can make his voice heard and
influence the course of human affairs. Local community groups and such organizations as Common
Cause are fast becoming channels through which
these concerns can become articulate and united.

The energy crisis which is a vast and ominous
cloud on the world horizon has made us take a new
look at America's total dependence on oil and the
automobile. We are beginning to see the folly, indeed
the immorality, of our prodigal waste of natural
fuels, the built-in obsolescence of American automobiles, and the enormous pollution of the atmosphere by the wasteful kinds of engines we use.
We are beginning to ask hard questions: Do we
need a hundred million automobiles in this land?
To what extent is our total life influenced by the
advertising of the great motor companies? Why
should a Christian family own two or more huge,
dangerous, overpowered, luxurious cars? Should we
not be looking favorably at public transportation,
smaller and more economical cars, bicycles and
even a return to walking?

Another significant breakthrough toward simplicity is in the field of architecture. It is only
dawning, but no longer do we consider the ultimate
in housing to be a vast, drafty, ornate house; nor do
we any longer admire huge Gothic-style churches.
Here the wave of the future is toward simpler, func-
tional styles, built of honest materials, which may
be far more comfortable to live in, work in, and
worship in. Here and there are architects like Paolo
Soleri who are dreaming of cities in which people
can live in freedom and cooperation, using energy
economically—a new vision of the "City of God."

New patterns of church life are emerging, with a

new and deeper appreciation of the New Testament church and of patterns which older generations found good. This is true in the area of church organization and polity. The ecumenical movement is concentrating on "grass roots" ecumenicity, instead of the creation of great monolithic bureaucracies. There is a trend in many parts of the world toward lively and creative "house churches" either within or outside the life of local congregations. A new appreciation of small groups in the congregation and of the potential strength of small and intimate congregations are supplanting the emphasis on bigness. No longer are huge bureaucratic congregations with thousands of children in Sunday school considered the most successful churches.

Multipurpose buildings which serve the community seven days a week and churches "in the round" are supplanting the huge and ostentatious edifices which fed local church pride and were used only a few hours a week. The church now in many places is seeking to return to its true function as servant and is expressing this sense of mission in its buildings. Church leaders are seeing anew that the church will endure and find its true being in simple, humble, and faithful obedience to Jesus Christ—and in structures which promote and express such obedience.

We are becoming more aware now of the diseases of affluence—greed, slavery to things, tyrannical technology, insidiously powerful advertising, shallow and immoral economy based solely on production growth, temptation to conspicuous consumption. And, at the same time, we are becoming more aware, through the worldwide coverage of the TV camera and tireless reporting in the news media, of the diseases of poverty, of lack of affluence. We are seeing—sometimes to the point of callousness—the malnutrition, the broken homes, the idleness, the crime, the despair, and the anger which are so widespread both in the city ghetto and in the rural slum. At both extremes of the scale, selfish affluence and grinding poverty, human life becomes degraded and brutish.

America and the world are reexamining their priorities. And in the process those who follow Jesus Christ enjoin the world to hear the admonition of this master of simple living to "set your mind on God's kingdom and his justice before everything else, and all the rest will come to you as well." That is the essence of Simple Living.

Chapter 1

THAT ALL MAY HAVE BREAD

WHEN MY DAUGHTER was small, she would often annoy her parents by refusing to eat some "perfectly good" food that was placed on her plate. When her mother reminded her that there were millions of starving children who would be glad for even the scraps she left, she would say, "Then why don't you give *them* this stuff?" How easy it is to oversimplify the problem of hunger. We say that a major motive for simple living is that if we simplify our wants for bread, fuel, clothing, goods of all kinds, there will be more for others. But the problem is far wider and deeper than simply loading ships with surplus grain and sending them to Africa or Bangladesh. Each of God's children should have enough to eat, land to cultivate, clothing for his children, housing for shelter, books and education, medical care—his just share of all the world's goods. But how can we help? Can we by self-denial increase the chances of our brother's having enough? How can just distribution be achieved?

Our concern that all may have enough has led us to a serious reevaluation of priorities. It is difficult for Americans to talk to the peoples of the developing nations about the need to limit the population and conserve resources, when they as a people have been so prodigally wasteful, and have as yet shown no signs of penitence or self-denial. The late Charles D. Bonsack of the Brethren used to say that we Americans are like a big boy at the table of a large family who takes on his plate half the potatoes, the biggest piece of ham, and the whole apple pie, then with knife and fork in hand defies the rest of the children to come and get any! Pastor Wilbur Liskey has well said that we are the only nation rich enough to bury ourselves in our own garbage.

Jason Bauserman has expressed our dilemma:

> The fact that the United States with 6% of the world's population uses about 50% of the world's goods and resources is extremely tormenting to me. That is nothing but pure greed. It is keeping others in the world poor and hungry. We have taken our share and theirs too. I believe this to be the main cause of war. In order to keep our high standard of living in this country, our economy is based to a large extent on waste (planned obsolescence, wasted energy, war material, waste paper, fancy packaging, etc.). What will be left for our children? Is there any doubt that Mammon has won out?

Desmond W. Bittinger writes:

> America consumes about nine times the world average of the world's products. America should voluntarily cut back and seek to help the others have more of the world's resources. But America must cut back for her own good also. Why should not the Brethren start?

Is the answer to expend our thought and energy to bring all the rest of the world up to our level of consumption? Bob Gross, a conscientious objector, writes from prison:

> The myth that some day the rest of the world will rise to the level of affluence now enjoyed in the United States and a few other countries is a lie. The tenuous ecological balance of this

planet is near to receiving a death blow just from the expansion/exploitation economy of the United States alone. It will not support such a standard of living for the whole human race. We must individually choose to live at such a level as could be maintained by the world's total population, or be guilty of stealing, in a very real way, from those who suffer for lack of those things we possess in wasteful abundance.

And a history professor, Robert A. Hess, adds this insight to the problem:

It is very important that we lead our people toward meaningful understandings of the simple life in light of the unethically disproportionate use of the world's raw materials in America, and in the context of the maiming effects on health of pollution, and in the context of prospective shortages which our consumption will create for our children. In this respect I believe it essentially Christian to restrain or reduce the American standard of living in order to lift the level of existence in other lands.

Kenneth M. Shaffer points out some dangers of our life-style.

Today's consumer economy attempts to cast out the simple life by deceiving us into believing we need everything that is available. It is obviously ridiculous to believe we need everything we see, yet ad men are making all kinds of headways.

There are two responses the person attempting to live the simple life can make to the intense consumerism of the American economy —total rejection or selective rejection. Those who practice total rejection, seeing the terrible

corrupt nature of the American economy, de-
cide to avoid all of it and retreat to life as it
was prior to the technological boom of the last
hundred years. Such is commendable and only
the bravest will attempt it. Unfortunately they
have to abandon the good with the bad. Proba-
bly they must forego electricity, yet electricity
is not in itself harmful. Actually it is helpful in
that it prolongs life, prevents blindness, aids
communication, etc. It seems wiser to ap-
proach electricity with selective rejection.
Rather than learning to live without electrici-
ty, learn to conserve it. Turn lights out when
they are not being used, use a hand can opener
rather than an electric one, use the air condi-
tioner only when you are working.

Brethren people like to eat well. And nothing
touches a Brethren person's heart more quickly
than a picture or a story of a child somewhere cry-
ing for bread or dying of malnutrition. They have
been quick to respond to the calls for famine relief.
They have taken seriously the New Testament injunction to feed the hungry, whether friend or foe.
We are now confronted with human needs and
hunger on an unprecedented scale. Specialists in
the field of world agricultural production and population pressures have been issuing predictions for
some years that in the 1970s there would be famine
in large areas of the world. We have come to take
such predictions with more seriousness than ever
before. In late 1973 we saw the continuing hunger
of Bangladesh and the apparent inability of the
weak, young government of the country to cope
with it. We saw the wide ravages of hunger in a
large part of India because of failure of the mon-
soon rains for several years in Maharashtra and
Central India. We saw the threat of severe famine

in the Sahel, a section of Africa as large as the entire United States with a population of twenty-five
million. Years of drought dried up the rivers, killed
most of the cattle, brought the Sahara Desert
hundreds of miles farther south into former savan-
nah country, and brought millions of people into
refugee camps.

Obviously we must find long-range solutions to
such problems. Even if we had the hundreds of ship-
loads of grain needed and could send them, we
could save some lives, but for what end, and for
what future? And how would the leavings on my
daughter's plate, or the savings of 200,000 frugal,
conscientious Brethren help in the long run? Here
is the rub: If we can persuade the American people
to quickly cut back their prodigal consumption,
would this create a depression so severe that they
would be still less able to help in the solution of
worldwide problems? And how can we relate to the
peoples of developing nations who view the acquisition of an automobile, a refrigerator, and a TV set as
the achievement of status once possessed only by
the affluent peoples of the West? How can we avoid
a patronizing attitude and yet be helpful? Crisis is
so imminent and the problems of achieving justice
and well-being so immense that we must seek radical solutions rather than temporary assuasions to
these great hurts and hungers of the world.

Do you remember the Shultz cartoon in which
Snoopy is shivering in deep snow? Charlie Brown
and Linus come out dressed in fine, warm jackets,
boots, mittens, and fur caps. As they stop by
Snoopy, Charlie Brown says, "Be of good cheer,
Snoopy, be warmed and fed." And Linus adds,
"Yes, Snoopy, be of good cheer!" This, unfortunate-
ly, represents the picture much of the world has of
America. Either we utter pious nonsense, rush to

provide short-term stopgap remedies, or cynically moralize that if the hungry people just had the gumption we have, they could, as we did, lift themselves by their own bootstraps. So arises the portrait of the "Ugly American."

If we are to be effective, we must begin to question some very widely held and deeply felt American assumptions. One is the belief that the light at the end of the tunnel is increasing bigness, growth, greater production and consumption, a never slackening acceleration of the Gross National Product. But the simple life does not see consumption as the key to the Kingdom at all. The American economy is so prodigally destructive of the basic resources—fossil fuels, water, soil, timber, minerals—that simply to encourage developing nations to follow our pattern would result in total exhaustion of all Earth's resources in a brief period of time. To continue to exploit the poorer nations, mining and buying their resources to maintain our own level of consumption, denying them the right to their proportionate share, is totally unrealistic. We must find some way in which all people together can come to a new understanding of what stewardship of the good Earth means. This will require that we in the affluent nations must give up many of our luxuries and much of what we consider to be the necessities of modern life. To give every family on Earth a car, a TV set, a full set of electric appliances and access to a beauty parlor simply won't do it; that would be suicidal.

A second assumption which should be questioned is that it will solve our problems if we try to export our capitalist, so-called free enterprise system. As Justice William O. Douglas has so well said, our present system is socialism for the rich and free enterprise for the poor. For as Toland, Fenton, and

McCulloch point out in a perceptive paper on world justice and peace, capitalism is by its very nature a system which promotes individualism, competition, and profit making with little or no regard for the social cost. It puts profits and private gain before social service and human needs. As such it is an unjust system which must be replaced.

If we are to do works of creative justice, kindness and charity, we need to work politically and associate ourselves with others who are concerned. We should be well informed about the World Health Organization and the Food and Agriculture Organization, and the studies and programs which they initiate. To do these things will in no way diminish participation in the organizations, such as Church World Service and CROP, which are doing so much around the world to alleviate hunger on both short-term and long-term bases. The Brethren have long carried a responsible share in supporting and leading such organizations. They are able to multiply and channel what individuals or local churches can do. Our goal should not be to simply give away what we have in vast quantity until others have as much as we have. Rather it should be to help the struggling people of the world to come to their full stature and dignity as human beings who can stand on their own feet and produce the necessities which they have every reason to believe are their right in a world created by a good God.

Harl Russell, retired Brethren General Board staff member in the field of gifts and money management, comments upon this larger vision in these words:

> *The simple life is a corrective to consumer extravagances. Developing countries should not be propagandized to buy or manufacture those products that do not contribute to the well-*

*being of the people. Liberation movements seek
to acquire for the deprived most of all the un-
needed materials. Our affluent society's conspicuous consumption and spectator extrava-
ganzas also misdirect those who seek a better
life for deprived peoples.*

We can take the lead in developing the attitude
that we ought not need or even desire the things
which the poor can never have. It staggers the mind
even to suggest the possibility that the United
States could ever become the kind of society in
which this norm would prevail. We at once begin to
say that this would lead to a dreary and homoge-
nous society on a level of bare subsistence. Our
present welfare systems are premised on the idea
that we want others to have what we have. But we
need to turn that thinking upside down. We can't
continue to have all we now have, even in this country. The world can never be fed at the American
standard of eating. This isn't a counsel of despair.
It is simply facing the fact that we in our country
have long been eating and using far more than our
share of everything.

The Church of the Brethren has a good record
from which we can start. We noted earlier that they
love to eat and to make sure that others eat. How
has this group tried to share on a global scale in the
past? When the Armenian people were driven from
their mountain land in the latter part of World War
I, the churches of America poured out money and
food on an unprecedented scale to succor these val-
iant Christian people. The Brethren were asked to
make a modest contribution. When the word got
around, the Brethren made such a generous contribution that they were at once asked to assist in the
administration of relief. The rest of the Christian
world was amazed at the generous response of this

small and little known sect. Then, after World War I had stirred the consciences of most church leaders, the Brethren began to pioneer in many ways. When Dan West was administering relief in Spain and saw the desperate hunger of children, he conceived the idea of the Heifer Project. Started by the Church of the Brethren, this imaginative organization has long been totally ecumenical. It has operated on principles which have made it a far-reaching and creative response to the problems of hunger. Church World Service, which has had so great an impact in all the lands ravaged and starved by World War II, was started by the prodding and challenging ecumenical ministry of M.R. Zigler. And when the World Council of Churches was struggling to unite the Protestant forces of the world, its ministry to the hungry and the refugees was again sparked by this dynamic Brethren leader.

Long before these dramatic excursions into practical service on an ecumenical scale, the overseas ministries of the Church of the Brethren were operating on a wide basis of service to the total hunger and need of man. In the early years of the Brethren's mission in India, the country was terribly devastated by famine, at its worst in Gujarat. With typical Brethren concern for the hungry, Brethren missionaries, backed by a compassionate outpouring of funds from the home church, started relief projects and orphanages which saved thousands of lives. The mission in China was likewise noted for compassionate sharing in times of famine and epidemic. Chalmer Faw, in evaluating the work of the Brethren in Nigeria, points out that this same down-to-earth concern for the whole man's well-being, has resulted in a ministry which includes healing, education, and rural uplift with a passionate presentation of the gospel. The Brethren in their missions and volunteer service relief activities have always seen the gospel as Christ himself proclaimed his mission in Luke 4, quoting from Deutero-Isaiah,

> The spirit of the Lord is upon me because he has anointed me;
>
> he has sent me to announce good news to the poor,
>
> to proclaim release for prisoners and recovery of sight for the blind;
>
> to let the broken victims go free,
>
> to proclaim the year of the Lord's favour
>
> (*Luke 4:18-19* NEB).

Perhaps no other person in the Church of the Brethren has given so much compassionate and creative thought to the world problems of hunger and the Christian response to these problems as has Ira W. Moomaw. Three notable books have come from his pen dealing with the problems: *To Hunger No More* (Friendship Press, 1963), *The Challenge of Hunger* (Frederick A. Praeger, 1966), and *Crusade Against Hunger* (Harper and Row, 1966). In this latter book, Moomaw quotes W. A. Visser t'Hooft, then General Secretary of the World Council of Churches:

> *In our times the basic problem of overcoming hunger and poverty and of social justice has become the issue which dominates all other issues, and on the solution of which the future of mankind depends.*

In his books, Moomaw tells the story of the agricultural missions movement in which he has played a most significant part. After many years as an agricultural and educational missionary in India, equipped with a Ph.D. from Ohio State and an inexhaustible compassion and resourcefulness, he became the executive secretary of Agricultural Missions, Inc. He held this post until his retirement. It is notable that he was succeeded in this post by another Brethren missionary, J. Benton Rhoades. Reading Ira Moomaw's books gives one the profound impression that here is a ministry being carried on in many countries of the world which on the most basic and Christian foundation is getting at the problem of hunger. After many years of service in most of the countries of the world where the church is working at the task of sharing bread in the most creative ways, Moomaw does not despair. He has seen hunger firsthand. Yet he believes that hope rises from the land. He sees hope in the indomitable courage of the farmers and peasants who are no longer content to believe that it is the will of God that they remain hungry, sick and poor:

It would be cruel and shortsighted to shut our eyes to the clouds that are rising over much of the world. Nevertheless, there is no cause for despair; indeed, there are reasons for hope.

Probably the brightest of them is the billion or more people in Asia, Africa and Latin America who have awakened to the vision of a new Earth where there will be food, medicine, books, shelter, and justice. I have met hundreds of these people in their homes, plowed with them in their fields, worshiped with them in their churches. They do not seek either power or luxury. They want only a chance to work. They will make any sacrifice, endure any hardship, to achieve their noble aim. They are hopeful; they are listening, not for the zero hour or the toll of midnight; but for the peal that will herald a new day.

Schooled in patience and by adversity, they do not expect to see miracles overnight. They do, however, ask for concrete and tangible assurance that the rest of the world cares. To work with these people no doubt presents to the churches their finest opportunity in history.

The second reason for hope is the progress we are making in technology. Twenty-five years ago, the demand of so many for a better life seemed so unattainable as to leave us hopeless. Today, we know that from a technical standpoint, at least, their cry can be answered.

We have yet to consider perhaps the greatest reason for hope. It is not generally realized that in Asia and Africa alone there are more than 120,000 organized Protestant congregations. They are served by 82,000 ministers. Seventy percent of these churches are located in villages in the midst of the greatest concentration of human need. I have often seen among these people acts of self-denial and faith that should shame those of us who live so comfortably. What the future could be if the affluent churches of the West were to uphold the hands of these people with adequately trained workers and material means on a self-help basis, so that each of these village churches could become a lighthouse of hope serving its community.

In another hour of our history President Lincoln declared, "We shall nobly save or meanly lose the last best hope of Earth."

God's plan that the Earth become a peaceful and kindly home for all mankind is clear. The prophets of old proclaimed it; the Lord gave his life for it. The "revolution of rising hope" in our time can be viewed as a part of that plan. This presents to the church a summons to mission that no other agency can fulfill. The mission is to express God's love and concern by means of great deeds as well as by words.

To respond to this summons in ways that will be acceptable to the host government and to the younger churches will require deep soul-searching as to our attitudes and the methods we employ. The situation calls for humbleness of spirit and a dedication of life and resources far beyond anything we have known thus far.

Thus, sharing in large and creative ways is both a major motivation for simple living, and a fruitful harvest of its practice. The Christian life-style of uncluttered simplicity will have a constant, compassionate concern for the hungry, the naked, the homeless, the refugees, the prisoner, the sick. By living the kind of simplicity we have been seeking to describe and advocate, we will have something to share, not only a cup of water and a loaf of bread given in the name of Christ, but a ministry which gets at the roots of the problems, and works toward permanent solutions. Living thus, we need no longer wring our hands in futile and frustrated agony, or weep in angry despair; we can go into a broken and hungry world with our hands filled with bread.

Chapter 2

TENANTS OF THE ALMIGHTY

ONE OF THE most perceptive agricultural econo-
mists of this century, Arthur Raper, wrote a re-
markable book entitled *Tenants of the Almighty*.
The title accurately describes our relationship to
creation. In this chapter, we shall examine the implications of this relationship to a Christian life-
style. Our basic principle is simple obedience to
God, as taught in Matthew 6:33. Since we put as
first priority the achievement of God's purposes,
the attainment of his *shalom* (well-being, whole-
ness) in the world, we will look at the whole created
world and its gifts as a sacred trust. It is well that
we take a fresh look at Genesis 1 and Psalm 24 as
the bases for the Judeo-Christian doctrine of divine
creation. "In the beginning God created the heaven
and the Earth." This is a statement of tremendous
reach involving the cosmos. It sets forth in few but
eloquent words the elemental fact that the forma-
tion of the created world lies above and before humankind, and that therefore it is not man's but
God's. We find ourselves upon Earth with many
other creatures, all part of a great system which,
since it is beyond us and superior to us, is divine.
Therefore we must regard Earth as good and indeed holy. Since it is God who created and sustains
Earth and who wills the ultimate and perfect
harmony of the whole creation, all of us, whether
we live close to the land or not, must seek God's

will and *shalom* in our relationship to the ultimate sources of all things.

The common supposition that the doctrine of creation means that we are the owner, who must subdue Earth and dominate all living creatures, has led us to the very edge of doom. Aldo Leopold, in the introduction to his beautiful *Sand County Almanac*, points out the shift which we must make in attitudes toward Earth:

> *Conservation is getting nowhere because it is incompatible with our Abrahamic concept of land. We abuse land because we regard it as a community belonging to us. When we see land as a community to which we belong, we may begin to use it with love and respect. There is no other way for land to survive the impact of mechanized man, nor for us to reap from it the aesthetic harvest it is capable, under science, of contributing to culture.*
>
> *That land is a community is the basic concept of ecology, of ethics. . . . Our bigger-and-better society is now like a hypochondriac, so obsessed with its own economic health as to have lost the capacity to remain healthy. The whole world is so greedy for more bathtubs that it has lost the stability necessary to build them, or even to turn off the tap. Nothing could be more salutary at this stage than a little healthy contempt for a plethora of material blessings.*

Everywhere in the world now we are seeing the dire results of our failure to treat Earth with love and respect. Walter Clay Lowdermilk, who was a devout prophet of Christian use of land, many years ago wrote what he called the 11th Commandment. He wrote it after spending years in the Near and Middle East as a land-use consultant and seeing the tragic effects of a thousand years of abuse of the land. Note how relevant it is to our needs now:

XI. Thou shalt inherit the holy Earth as a faithful steward, conserving its resources and productivity from generation to generation. Thou shalt safeguard thy fields from soil erosion, thy living waters from drying up, thy forests from desolation, and protect thy hills from overgrazing by thy herds, that thy descendants may have abundance forever. If any shall fail in this stewardship of the land, thy fruitful field shall become sterile stony ground and wasting gullies, and thy descendants shall decrease and live in poverty or perish from off the face of the Earth.

When Astronaut Frank Borman looked back at Earth from the moon, he wrote his impressions: "I thought, how small; how small; how fragile; how beautiful!" It is only in very recent times that we are seeing how very fragile Earth is and how near we have come to destroying it with our wasteful exploitation of its soil, water, forests, streams, lakes, oceans, air, and the myriad forms of life which teem upon it. In the book, *To Love or To Perish*, anthropologist Margaret Mead has said:

I think we now have a global vision that is entirely different from any we have ever had before. In the past, each citizen in each nation cared most for his own country. Whether he abused it, strip-mined it, wrecked it and got a dust bowl, it was his own country, his own land. Now that we are dealing with whole continents, oceans and the global atmosphere, the limited local or national vision is meaningless. For the first time we have a chance of transcending tribal visions. When we see that life depends on saving the environment of life, and

*only when we fear for the safety of our own
grandchildren and other grandchildren, will we
care enough to do what we must to save the
whole planet. This offers a new Christian vision of stewardship: of land that must be
shared, air and oceans that must be shared—
or we will all suffer great loss together.*

Concern for environment is not new. In AD 61
Seneca wrote:

*As soon as I had gotten out of the heavy air of
Rome and from the stink of the smoky chim-
neys thereof, which, being stirred, poured forth
whatever pestilent vapors and soot they held
in them, I felt an alteration of my disposition.*

And diarist John Evelyn in 1661 described the
"hellish and dismal cloud of sea coal so universally
mixed with the air that London's inhabitants
breathe nothing but impure and thick mist . . . so
that catarrhs, coughs, and consumptions rage more
in this city than in the whole Earth besides."

In many parts of the world there are evidences of
great civilizations which rose and flourished and
fell. Often the cause of decline and fall was not conquest from without, but the exploitation and destruction of the fertile soil which was the basis for a
populous and advanced civilization. This has been
true in the Middle East, in Central America, and in
many other areas. In this country, the early settlers
found a rich and fertile land. Ignoring the intimate
relationship of land and people which many of the
Indians had developed, the settlers charted a
course for our country in which streams that once
ran clear would silt up. Billions of tons of the best
topsoil would be carried to the seas by the great,
but filthy rivers. The fish would die, the land would
erode and be scarred by gullies. The rich elements
necessary for lush vegetation would be leached

from the soil. Forests and mountain slopes would be denuded. Farms would become less and less productive and finally abandoned.

When some spectacular results of untrammeled exploitation and destruction would begin to appear, such as the complete extinction of the passenger pigeon and the near destruction of the bison, and vast forest and prairie fires swept the lands, people would begin to awaken. President Theodore Roosevelt and Gifford Pinchot started the conservation movement. Such concerned naturalists as Henry David Thoreau, John Muir, Aldo Leopold and Jay "Ding" Darling agitated for preservation of the wilderness and its endangered flora and fauna. Conservation laws were passed, national parks and forests were established. The Civilian Conservation Corps, the Soil Conservation Service, the Tennessee Valley Authority—all were steps in national awareness and growing concern.

Where have the Brethren been in these movements? During the years when the most widespread exploitation and destruction were going on unchecked, most Brethren were farmers. For the most part, they were good stewards of the land, although there were some who exploited the soil and wasted it as irresponsibly as their neighbors. Now many areas where the Brethren once had strong communities and churches have been abandoned to agribusiness. The churches have moved to town as the youth of Brethren families have left their rural homes and heritage to become a part of the mainstream of urban American life. There are, however, a significant number of rural communities where the Brethren still are in the forefront of their life and work. Strong rural churches and their constituent communities exist in Pennsylvania, Maryland, Virginia, Ohio, Indiana, Iowa, Kansas and California. In some of these areas it is becoming increasingly difficult for a young man to start farming or for anyone to maintain a family farm.

R. Truman Northup, Brethren district executive, expresses his concern:

> Unless they inherit or own the land, the Brethren cannot afford to buy sufficient land and equipment to make a living, pay farming expenses and the mortgage payments. There would be a possibility if several were to work together in a corporation or a cooperative, but the competition with agribusiness in the present tax structure makes this very difficult.

On the other hand, Leon Neher, a farmer-college professor in Kansas, answers the question of whether Brethren can be good farmers today:

> That's what we're trying to do and I hope we can pull it off. Via further intensification of program rather than extension of it many more can do it!

Dr. and Mrs. Ira Moomaw share this opinion:

> We could and should be [good farmers]. Our institutions too often steered young people away. We seemed to underrate our rural heritage. We have so far not trained ministers to operate effectively as informed leaders in rural churches. What should we do? Study more deeply. Almost none of our church literature, retreats or other occasions deal with this. Our leaders would not appear to be adequately informed as to the new developments in rural life.

But recognizing the inescapable fact that most Brethren, as well as most other American Christians, no longer live on farms or have any significant relationship to the land, what then can we do? We can recognize that we are "tenants of the Almighty" where we live; aware of our own share of responsibility for the preservation and reverent use of the good Earth.

Leona S. Dick, a Brethren woman who is a teacher and homemaker, writes:

> I try to live close to nature, to simplify life in an ongoing process. We who are city dwellers may have a yard or a garden where we can spend many happy hours planting, weeding, pruning, and enjoying the splendor of growing things. Or we may be apartment dwellers where potted plants must substitute for a garden.

Ida S. Howell, a retired professor, writes:

> This depends on one's definition of "good." Do we mean efficient or successful? Yes, I think they [the Brethren] could be good farmers, especially on small farms or cooperatives, though they can hardly make a living today because of regulations. They cannot become wealthy, but I assume that isn't essential!

Melanie May, a thoughtful student, comments thus upon the Brethren's relationship to Earth:

> As farmers the Brethren lived intimately with creation and the natural world. They cared for the Earth and reaped its harvest for food and clothing. By being so involved in this part of God's world they had time to enjoy other parts also. Life was slower and simpler and so a person was not so involved as to shut out the guidance of God. Today we as Brethren still have a mission as farmers. Persons concerned for the creation and Earth are needed to provide food and care for the soil. Farm land is still rich in Pennsylvania, Virginia, Nebraska, Kansas, Indiana and Iowa. Yet the time is rapidly coming when we Brethren must stand for the importance of farm land and the fulfill-

*ment of rural living, because industry is rapid-
ly moving into the eastern sections of the
Brotherhood. We must witness to our concern
and to our heritage in the land, and delve into
the rich life which ties together Earth and man
to God.*

To be a good steward of the land means much
more than a passing interest in gardening, or beau-
tification of the roadside. It means seeing the intimate and inviolable relationship of the whole creation under God. We must learn to see the whole of
the creation as a pyramid. The base is the soil, the
land. The next layer is all of plant life. Dependent
and feeding upon this plant layer is the animal
world with many layers, man being near the top, an
omnivorous creature along with the bear, the rac-
coon, the squirrel. And finally are the carnivores.
All are interdependent upon the others. We cannot
waste or destroy any part of this complex without
serious harm to the whole. We are under a moral
and religious obligation to be good members of this
total community which includes all creation from
the soil and the ocean to the most perceptive beings. The land ethic, as Aldo Leopold points out,
enlarges the boundaries of the community of which
we are members to include soil, water, plants, and
animals, or collectively, the land.

It is surely incumbent upon all who would be
good stewards of Earth to work hard at eliminating
pollution and stemming the tides of destructive and
wasteful exploitation. What are some things we can
do? Allen Deeter, college professor, suggests:

*We should not use phosphate cleaners. We
should protest any local factories or sewage
and other disposal systems which do not conform with good ecological practices. We should*

buy cars which do not wear out and drive them longer than most people do. We should urge an end to tearing down perfectly good buildings simply to build bigger or more economically productive buildings on the same sites. We should work at repairing and reusing clothing, passing it on to friends, rather than simply giving it or throwing it away. I do not think pollution is as much of a problem as good total use of the world's resources. I also think that we should limit our families and encourage the use of birth control methods. We must first start as Brethren, as Americans, as an example.

Dorris Blough tells of her experience:

Brethren can buy automobiles that use less gas. I personally refuse to accept paper sacks in stores, preferring boxes that can be reused. There is a long list of "waste reduction" steps that the individual can take. Even as a child I was very conscious of not throwing anything out of the windows of the car. I am director of the local recycling collection center. Recycling is certainly a part of the answer, but waste reduction is the other. Using less power is something we talk about but do little about.

Leon Neher challenges:

Buy/use smaller cars, buy/use only what food, clothing, shelter we really need, recycle everything possible; share whatever items of our livelihood, e.g. cars, machinery, etc., we can; use agricultural chemicals sparingly and with deep respect; help to decentralize industry and population into "village industries," etc. Our town [Quinter, Kansas] has several small industries—the kind that make sense both ecologically and sociologically.

One young Brethren couple has taken this whole matter very seriously. They have bought an old farm in the mountains of West Virginia and are building their own house. Eventually they plan to raise all their own food organically, pipe cold spring water into the house, produce their own fuel from a woodlot, use only what electricity they can produce by windmill or some other homemade device. They hope to be able to live a full, rich life without the aid of telephone or TV. They tell of an older couple, ages 70 and 90, who spend four hours a day on "bread labor" with the rest of their time spent on reading, writing, playing music, visiting, etc.

This young couple, Mr. and Mrs. Jason Bauserman, former Brethren Volunteer Service workers, think that being "good farmers" trapped many Brethren and Mennonite people into making too much money and yielding to materialism.

Aware of the devastation wrought by chemical sprays, insecticides, defoliants, and inorganic fertilizers, many young Brethren are turning to organic farming and gardening. Others are examining this life-style and their relationship to the good Earth.

A sound "theology of ecology" is based squarely upon the Christian doctrine of creation and an understanding of our partnership with God in our use of the land. Some passages from the New Testament bear upon the matter of our relationship to Earth.

St. Paul's profound statement in Romans 8:19-23 (NEB) speaks of God's ultimate purpose that not only humankind but the whole universe share in the redemption Christ brings:

> *For the created universe waits with eager expectation for God's sons to be revealed. It was made the victim of frustration, not by its own*

choice, but because of him who made it so; yet
always there was hope, because the universe it-
self is to be freed from the shackles of mortali-
ty and enter upon the liberty and splendour of
the children of God. Up to the present, we
know, the whole created universe groans in all
its parts as if in the pangs of childbirth. Not
only so, but even we, to whom the Spirit is
given as firstfruits of the harvest to come, are
groaning inwardly while we wait for God to
make us his sons and set our whole body free.

The letter to the Ephesians echoes the concept
that the whole creation, which has been despoiled
and placed in bondage by the sin of man, will in
God's good time be made perfectly whole again.
And finally, the Revelation speaks in glowing terms
of the ultimate consumation of God's purposes,
when there shall be a "new Heaven and a new
Earth."

So the Christian life-style, based upon loyal obedience to the sovereign will of God and dedicated to
his *shalom,* will display a deep, loving, appreciative
respect and even reverence for the good Earth. We
who seek to live by this life-style will resolutely
turn away from any practices which waste, despoil,
exploit, hoard or destroy God's good gifts of soil,
water, plant and animal life, and air. We will live on
Earth as joint heirs with all of God's creatures in
the grace of life.

Chapter 3

LIVING IN COMMUNITY

THE BRETHREN'S discomfort with the hectic 20th-century life-style they inherited, shared by many others, has led to much creative thought and dialog. Many serious youth have boldly struck out into new patterns of living—a few in Christian communes such as Reba Place Fellowship in Evanston, Illinois, or the Bruderhof (Society of Brothers). Others are doing courageous and creative thought and experimentation in the hope of combining the best of past and present life-styles.

The Brethren are aware with Thomas Wolfe that "you can't go home again." Kermit Eby, one-time Brethren leader in the labor movement, discovered perceptively that, as much as he loved and honored his beloved Baugo, Indiana, he could not go back to it. We all are making that observation. But there are sturdy values in the Brethren heritage which can be recaptured; there are biblical imperatives in this background which ought to be explored and followed. We cannot go back to our Baugo or Paradise Prairie, or Singers Glen; but we can try to rediscover the basic principles in a heritage which are good and universal.

Ever since the beginning of the Christian movement in Jerusalem, there have been experiments in living in community as a way of simplifying and enhancing life. The accounts of life in the primitive church (Acts 2:44, 45 and 4:32-37) tell of the community of goods practiced by the church and the spirit in which it was carried out. These first Christians believed that Jesus called people to show their love for God and neighbor in practical ways of love. The church was to be the actual demonstration of what life in the perfect Kingdom of God would be. All barriers of rank, social position, wealth or poverty were broken down. Love which was willing to surrender everything was the Christian's hallmark. Nothing was too costly for these Christians when the common interest of the surrendered community was at stake, and the church developed an incredible activity in works of real charity. The church had a deep and loving interest in the poor, the widow, the orphan and the disinherited. Everything the church owned, they believed, belonged to the poor. Their affairs were the business of the church. The spirit of voluntary giving was a basic feature of the movement. In this primitive church the spontaneity of genuine love merged private property into a communism of love.

It does not appear from New Testament accounts that the churches established in other areas followed this communal pattern, although they maintained the same deep concern for works of charity, for caring for the poor and the widow. These concerns were translocal. When food shortages and the increasing stream of pilgrims coming to Jerusalem placed severe strain upon the resources of the mother church, the apostle Paul organized a relief collection among the many Gentile churches, and he personally led the group carrying this significant gift to Jerusalem. This was a means of cementing the sundered churches which were of such diverse origins, as well as of bringing practical relief to the poor members of the Jewish church. Although the communal pattern did not spread widely, the basic principle of loving responsibility among all members of the church, and even with the poorest of their neighbors, was everywhere characteristic of the growing church.

Since the First Century there have been sporadic efforts to recreate the communalism of the primitive church. Such movements as Montanism in the Second Century, the revolutionary movements of justice and love inspired by Arnold of Brescia, were early manifestations of the movement. The Waldensians, the itinerant community founded by Francis of Assisi, the Bohemian and Moravian Brethren, the Brothers of the Common Life, the Beguines and the Beghards, and then finally the early Anabaptist* communities all exhibited more or less the communal way of life. Many of the Roman Catholic orders have exhibited the best features of Christian communal living, emphasing voluntary poverty, sharing all revenues for the sake of their mission and obedience to Christ.

Communal experimentation for the sustaining of a simple life-style has not been confined to the Christian church and its sects. History is filled with accounts of secular utopias, some of which attracted many persons for a time, but which foundered on the failure to provide the motivation of selfless *agape* love. In our own generation, there has been a rash of communal experiments. Many communes have sprung from the counterculture. Some are shelters for a rabble of disillusioned and untram-

---

* A religious sect which arose in Zurich in 1523, which advocated the restoration of primitive Christianity, and which held that infant baptism was scripturally unwarranted, that there should be no union of church and state, and that Christians should renounce private possessions and practice a religious communalism.

meled rebels who irresponsibly throw overboard
most of the accepted mores of society. Others are
sincere and honest efforts to build a new and ideal-
istic community, free from the ills of modern ma-
terialistic and competitive life. In some, there are
creative and innovative attempts to find new life-
styles of marriage and family. Some are attempts to
come to terms with the land, communities which re-
vert to subsistence farming, usually organic.

There have also been widespread and short-term
popular movements to "share the wealth" through
political or other means. In this country, several
such movements had their origins in the days of the
Great Depression. The Townsend Plan, Huey
Long's Share Our Wealth clubs, Father Coughlin's
National Union for Social Justice, and Upton Sin-
clair's EPIC movement, all were more or less frantic efforts to share wealth and to distribute resources more justly.

It may be profitable for us to examine briefly
some of the communal ventures which seek to re-
store the New Testament church patterns and to
learn what we can from them. Perhaps the oldest of
these is the Hutterite movement. It is one of the
earliest of the Anabaptist societies and is thriving
today in strong religious agricultural communities
in Western United States and Canada. These communities maintain stable family life, rigid rules for
membership and real community of property. Many
of the communities are quite prosperous, practicing
modern agriculture, using the most modern farming
implements, and often producing large quantities of
superior products for market. The communities
maintain strict isolation from the outside world and
have often incurred the enmity of their neighbors
because of their isolation, their pacifist stance, and
their evident prosperity. Since their families are

usually rather large and few youth leave the community, there is steady and healthy growth in the movement.

The Shakers, officially known as the United Society of Believers in Christ's Second Appearing, came to America from England in 1774. They believed in celibacy, sex equality, separation from the world, hard and creative work, and community of property. Because of their skills in agriculture, fine craftsmanship and their moral purity, their communes were successful for many years. However, they are now almost extinct.

The Amana Colonies in Iowa were for nearly a hundred years the most successful religious communes in America. Founded as the Community of True Inspiration in Southern Germany, they migrated to Western New York, and then to Iowa. While they still have a strong church community, they are now organized as a corporation, manufacturing nationally known appliances of high quality.

To a lesser extent communities of Amish and Mennonite people have exhibited the characteristics of communal life.

The "Bruderhof" or Society of Brothers, started some fifty years ago in Germany by a young Ph.D. scholar and youth movement secretary named Eberhard Arnold, was driven out of Germany by the Nazi movement. The group settled for a time in England, then in the bitter years of World War II moved to Paraguay. The move to the United States took place in 1954. At present, the society has two major centers in this country—Rifton, New York, and Farmington, Pennsylvania—and one in Sussex, England. In the 1950s the community attracted several young Brethren families, most of whom are still active in the movement. The society has an excellent printing press, the Plough Publishing House, and manufactures a line of well-designed, creative toys. This society strongly emphasizes wholesome family living, purity of life, creative work, complete dedication to following Jesus, and total community of property. Eberhard Arnold wrote in the classic apology of the Society, "Why We Live in Community," in 1927:

> That we live in community and work in community is an inescapable necessity for us. We must carry through this common life as that which determines everything we do or think. No kind of designed effort or exertion has been driving us on this way. Rather a certainty has come over us, a certainty that springs from the source for all of life's necessities. This source of power we confess to be in God. All life, which he has created, exists in community and is directed toward community. For this reason, we too must live in community. . . .
>
> We have only one weapon to fight the depravity of conditions of life today. The weapon of the Spirit is constructive work in the community of love. We recognize no sentimental love, no love without work. . . .
>
> Whatever the individual acquires in the way of income or property, large or small, is unconditionally given in to the common life by every member of the circle who holds responsibility. But even the community as a committed group does not regard itself as the owner of its enterprises, its goods and chattels. Rather, the community group acts as trustee for the goods and valuables for the community of all, and for that reason holds the door open for all and demands for all decisions an unclouded unanimity in one Spirit.

In her new book, *Your Experience and the Bible*, Anna B. Mow writes of the Society of Brothers:

> *For the past seventeen years our son Merrill has been with the Society of Brothers. Of course, that caused me to be sincerely interested. From the first I was satisfied on my two main concerns: was it Christ-centered and was it family-centered? Through the centuries many communal efforts were merely sociological in goal, even more were so ascetic that they had no room for families. Others included families, but the family was not a responsible central unit. I am so thankful that our grandchildren in this community have the security of a family of their very own, but also the security of the love of the larger family of God.*
>
> *After fifty years of growth, difficulties, and blessings, this group still testifies by its words and its life that God lives, that he has a will for us, that he and his will are revealed in the life, death, and resurrection of Jesus of Nazereth, and that he makes his will known to all who seek him. This is their only goal and the sole reason for living in community.*

A more recent and quite different approach to total and intentional Christian community is that of Reba Place Fellowship in Evanston, Illinois. This group was intentionally established in a metropolis and is much more open to the tides of modern metropolitan life than is the more insulated Bruderhof. We quote from their own account of how the fellowship came to be and what they are undertaking to be and do:

> *In the early 1950's a group of seminary students and relief workers who had been in Europe after the war were deeply challenged by the rediscovery of ancient Anabaptist*

thought which was taking place at Goshen College in Indiana. As original documents of this Sixteenth-Century Christian movement came to light, an exciting vision of the church took shape—a concept of the church as a disciplined brotherhood, determined to be radically obedient to Christ whatever the cost, and intensely evangelistic through the witness of its life.

A small group of young couples began to discuss the implications of this vision for their own lives. They longed for deeper meaning than they found in much contemporary church life. The example of the earliest church communities, particularly as recorded in the book of Acts, stirred a response in their hearts. If the apostles who walked with Jesus and were led by his Spirit were compelled to take his teachings so literally, maybe that was what was expected of anyone who would be Christ's disciple. The group of young people also noted that throughout church history others who sought to follow the dynamic way of love taught by Christ were often led to form communities where sharing both spiritually and materially was carried out to a unique degree.

More than 135 of us intentionally live within walking distance of each other here in Evanston, Illinois. We feel it is more important to be near each other than to be near our jobs, special neighborhood or any other things. We share a common treasury because we see the needs of our brothers and sisters as our own. We're each part of a whole—not separate, not going in different directions. By the same unity of life we share our decisions, seeking first the Kingdom of God in all that we do.

Some of our households have been extended to include more than a single nuclear family. We seek to live in peace and nonviolence.

We have found that a subtle enslavement to possessions persists even for the "generous" person. Christ did not call for mere generosity; he asked his followers to renounce the "right" to all we own. In our Fellowship we ask all our members to cultivate that inner detachment from things which will make a just and equitable sharing of goods possible. To facilitate this we have adopted the practice of Jesus and his twelve disciples and the practice of the early Jerusalem church of a common treasury to which we bring our economic assets and earnings. From this treasury each member receives a living allowance based on current welfare standards, as well as support for other necessities such as housing and medical expenses. Fellowship funds in excess of what is needed for the support of its various members and guests are then distributed elsewhere.

Members of these modern intentional communities would not insist that their way of life is for all Christians. Yet they believe they have found for themselves and for their families a way of life that comes as near as possible to fulfilling the demands of Christ for total discipleship, and that their communities are a witness to what the church at its best can and ought to be. Al Jennings, young Brethren activist, comments upon the need for closer community, based upon his own observation of Reba Place:

My vision of community is closely related to my vision for the church. It stems from the Christian imperative to begin living here and now a radically new way as a sign of the com-

ing new Kingdom. We bring about change in the larger society by first changing our own personal lives. By receiving nurture and strength in our smaller community, we are able to go beyond ourselves, to witness to the larger society and attempt to bring greater justice among the members of the human family.

It is impossible to live in a radical way in this society as long as we stay isolated in nuclear families. . . . We need to move toward closer cooperation and sharing with others. The more people who live together and the more closely material goods are shared, the more economical the household. . . .

Intentional community can only be successful if the intentions of the various members are well in tune, compatible and in good balance. It is important that prospective members know each other well and commitments are made on common foundations.

Bethany Theological Seminary professor Donald Miller makes these pertinent comments on communal life:

I am especially familiar with the Bruderhof. I am very much impressed with much of what they do. I would like to see some of that incorporated into our regular way of living. I would myself find the community oppressive in terms of individual expression. Such expression they consider to be offensive against the Spirit. I believe that the Spirit can show itself in a kind of individuality that they do not allow. Nevertheless, there is a great deal about the Bruderhof that I find very attractive.

Professor Ken Brown of Manchester College writes his observations:

I spent a month studying various communal

> *groups in the Northeast; I have studied utopian*
> *literature. Any large group needs disciplined,*
> *authoritative leadership, common values, a re-*
> *ligious base. (The Icarians are considered the*
> *one successful U.S. group without a religious*
> *base, but their strong communistic commit-*
> *ment served as a deep religious foundation in*
> *the Tillichian sense.) Bruderhof provides the*
> *classic case study. It is not spiritually liberat-*
> *ing, though it does solve many "simple life"*
> *problems. It shifts idolatry from self to com-*
> *munity.*

Finally, minister Robert H. Hess, who has visited
and observed several communities, comments:

> *They provide a lot of learning for us straight,*
> *middle Americans on to how to share, how to*
> *live simply and healthily; and probably more*
> *happily."*

What then can we do to apply some of the values
which are stressed by the intentional Christian
communes? In the first place, their emphasis upon
total commitment and simple obedience to Jesus in
all things is the very heart of the Brethren concept
of the simple, uncluttered life-style.

The complete concern for the best welfare of the
total group stands in sharp contrast to the apathy
and reluctance to be involved with one another and
with our world which is so characteristic of most
congregations. Pastor Olden Mitchell writes:

> *It is possible and desirable, essential in a*
> *sense, to live simply today. It may be neces-*
> *sary to develop some form of cooperative, some*
> *variety of communal concern and sharing to*
> *freely achieve the simple life today. It will be*
> *very difficult for one person or one family to*
> *pursue the simple life alone without a group*
> *support of love and caring.*

When a local congregation lives in close community, it becomes aware of and sensitive to the human needs of every family and individual in its community of faith.

Charles Boyer, Volunteer Services Director for the Church of the Brethren, proposes a Center for Life Study for the church. This might well provide guidance for many people, as youth or families after living and working in the center for a period of time, to return home to share insights with their local congregations.

Certainly one very practical application of the principles of Christian community would be for neighbors and fellow church members to share many of their tools and conveniences. Why should every family on a block or in a small community own its own lawn mower, fertilizer spreader, or slide projector? There are many imaginative, practical steps in sharing which we can take which are ecologically, economically, and religiously sound.

Not many of us are likely to move into the kind of intentional Christian communities we have alluded to in this chapter. But we can and must find practical ways to make their loving concern and richness of shared life operative in our home and community.

Chapter 4

A PLAIN PEOPLE

THE BRETHREN for the first two hundred years of their history were counted among the "plain people." They held firmly to the conviction that a plain, simple and uncluttered life-style was a gospel virtue.

The Brethren were usually good farmers, frugal, industrious and temperate. But like many of their neighbors, some Brethren exploited and despoiled their land and then moved on to repeat the process.

The expansion of the church often came about through migration of colonies of Brethren seeking new areas of fertile agricultural land.

Farms were usually self-contained. Money was scarce, and most foods, fiber for clothing, and materials for shelter were produced and processed at home. The houses of the Brethren were sturdy, large, and of a simple, dignified architecture, reminiscent of their ancestral homes in Germany and Switzerland. Their meetinghouses were plain and solidly built, reflecting their pattern of church life. As Brethren moved into new areas, the leading families often built spacious living rooms separated by movable partitions so that space could be provided for congregational meetings. Sometimes twenty or thirty years would elapse before a congregation would build its meetinghouse. Many such houses are extant and occupied by Brethren today. One conspicuous example is Tunker House,

at Broadway, Virginia, once the home of theologian
Peter Nead, and the birthplace of Brethren ecumenical leader M. R. Zigler.

In colonial America and through most of the
19th Century, the Brethren were almost universally
included among the "plain" sects in American
church life. Mennonites, Amish, Brethren, Quakers,
and several smaller groups, such as the Brethren in
Christ (River Brethren) and Schwenkfelders, made
up a substantial part of the population of the
southern half of Pennsylvania and large portions of
Maryland, Virginia, Ohio and Indiana. Melvin
Gingerich writes in his book, *Mennonite Attire
Through Four Centuries:*

> *During recent years, thousands of American
> tourists have visited Lancaster County, Penn-
> sylvania, to observe a segment of America's
> "plain people," and possibly many have gone
> back to New York and other cities with only a
> superficial understanding of why these fellow
> citizens, whose ancestors have been in this
> country for over two centuries, have not been
> completely absorbed in the American melting
> pot but instead have retained their simple
> dress and their simple style of life. A definition
> of terms and a discussion of the motives of the
> "plain people" will help to answer these ques-
> tions. The term "plain people" is used to refer
> to those whose dress is plain and simple in con-
> trast to the "gay people" who follow the
> changing, popular styles of the average groups
> in American society. Don Yoder wrote earlier
> of the* Plain Dutch *and* Gay Dutch: Two
> Worlds in the Dutch Country, *The "plain
> Dutch" are the Mennonites, Amish, Brethren,
> and related sectarian groups while the "gay
> Dutch" are particularly the Lutheran and Re-*

formed groups. The term "gay" and "plain" originated among the Quakers but it is perhaps the Mennonites who have perpetuated their use in Pennsylvania.

The combination of a rugged environment and a biblical concern for a simple following of Christ in all things created a frugal, relatively uncluttered and unsophisticated style of living. The simple life was for most Brethren an economic and social necessity, and they considered it a Christian virtue. As time went on, the attractions of affluence began to threaten the life-style which once had been a baptized necessity. Then, lest the advantages of maintaining unity in the church and a "gospel simplicity" be lost, the Brethren fell into a legalism which turned the outward forms of simple living into rigid membership requirements. Thus there came a flood of rules and legislative Annual Conference decisions which canonized the forms of simple living.

The Brethren have moved farther and more swiftly away from their identity with the "plain people" than the other groups mentioned in Gingerich's book.

The struggle through the Brethren's Annual Conference discussion and legislation for maintaining simplicity on a "dress question" agitated the church for a century. Not only the increasingly rigid prescription of a special garb, but such matters as the manner of wearing the hair and beard, the use of ornaments and the wearing of gold— all were subjects of agonizing debate and restrictive rules. Based on such scriptures as 1 Timothy 2:9 and 1 Peter 3:3, rigid decisions were handed down forbidding the use of gold watches and gold-framed eye glasses. The wearing of any kind of jewelry was long strictly forbidden.

Gradually forms of dress, which at one time were

not too distinguishable from the clothing worn by the neighbors of the Brethren, were adopted as prescribed and unchanging forms. Frederick Denton Dove, in *Cultural Changes in the Church of the Brethren*, has a good summary of the rise of the "dress question" in the church:

> The most visible evidence of firm belief in the doctrine of the simple life among the Brethren is in regard to dress. Their manner of dress early in their history became their distinctive mark of religious affiliation and at the same time of separation from the world of other men.
>
> There is no evidence that a particular style of dress was adopted by these people at the very beginning of the sect. It may be inferred, from their beliefs in opposition to vain show and out of economy, that their mode of dress bespoke simplicity. But it is highly probable that the form of dress was adopted from their early contact with the Quakers and Mennonites as a sort of mark of distinction for all nonresisting sects. Thus the plain, straight-brim hats for men and bonnets for women became the mode. As nonresistant principles became more pronounced at the outbreak of the Civil War, distinctive dress became more pronounced, and they cherished the modes which marked the dividing line between them and people in public life. The accepted style of clothes for men, besides plain hats, became coats and vests buttoned all the way to the neck, or rather hooked to the neck, for even buttons were prohibited among the colonial Brethren. Their coat collars were straight with no lapels, and neckties were worldly luxuries in apparel never to be worn. Women wore bonnets, the evolution of which is an interesting

*study in cultural change. . . . It was the custom
for women to wear under their bonnets a small
white "cap" of very thin material when attending worship services and to remove the bonnet
upon entering the church house and wear only
the "cap," known also as the prayer covering.
Capes were customary among the women of
the church and dresses were of the plainest
kind. No ruffles or colorful touches could be
worn. Trimmings of white, or lace collars, or
low necks were considered worldly and were
not tolerated. Jewelry was out of the question,
and gold was a "signal to Satan."*

Esther Fern Rupel, who has done a perceptive
study of Brethren dress in her doctoral thesis,
points out the rapid changes which were already
started at the turn of the century:

*By 1900 the walls of isolation were crumbling,
increasing the vulnerability of the way of life
of the Brethren to outside influences transmit-
ted by new communication and transportation
media. An evangelistic spirit among the membership and educated clergy and laity, located
both in rural and urban settings, resulted in
changes in the life of the church and in views
held by the membership. Changes were reflected in the prescribed dress and its significance.
Both the Brethren and the sisters gradually
laid aside items of clothing which signified
church membership and adopted items of fash-
ionable dress. . . .*

Dr. Rupel gives the history of the emphasis
upon dress codes among the Brethren as a large
part of the simple life emphasis. Explaining how
these matters became so important, she writes:

*Rather than adapting to social changes about
them, the Brethren clung to a mode of life*

which soon became the past. In time they found that this way of life was in opposition to that of the world. The Brethren strove to express their beliefs in every aspect of daily living. Their "plain dress" became a visual statement of their beliefs. As they sought unity within the group, the wide variations in this plainness became an issue. "Nonconformity to the world" came to mean conformity to the mode of dress worn by the group.

It seems clear that for at least a century after the founding of the church, while simplicity and frugality of life and modesty in dress were cardinal ethical positions of the church, there was no prescribed garb. The Brethren wore clothing similar to that of most of their neighbors in their class of society. But as time went on, the geographical expansion of the Brethren brought them into contact with other ethnic and social groups. To maintain their unity, and their distinctness from the world, they began to place more emphasis upon prescribed garb and to legislate ways to preserve "gospel simplicity." The power and authority of the Annual Conference, or Yearly Meeting, grew stronger and much time was given to discussion of questions coming from the churches having to do with the maintenance of the simple style of life. Dr. Rupel points out that there are over one hundred entries in the minutes of Annual Conference on dress alone. While it fell to the local church authorities to carry out the mandates of Annual Conference, the decisions of the Conference were considered binding. She writes:

The authority for a governing body within the church was taken from the New Testament. The rules of Annual Meeting were based upon the scriptures and were not of human design. Therefore the rules of Annual Meeting were

*considered to be obligatory and were to be
made a test of fellowship until such time as
changes were made according to Article 1 in
1860. Brethren differing in opinion were not to
teach contrary to the rules, but were to bring
the matter before the church for reconsid-
eration. Changes were to be made in the rules
only if they brought practice in closer
harmony with the gospel, according to Article
18 in 1880. If the scriptures were silent on an
issue then Annual Meeting could advise only
and not rule.*

Were there real values in this insistence on prescribed garb for the Brethren, which Annual Conference tried so strenuously to maintain? Bethany
Theological Seminary professor Dr. Donald Durnbaugh says:

*The costume was a witness in itself to a reli-
gious ethic. It immediately identified the
wearer as belonging to a group not identical
with the predominant culture. It saved time by
eliminating choices about what clothes to
wear. It indicated that all members of the
group were on the same level, as there were no
class differences signaled by dress.*

A longtime pastor, Clarence B. Fike, who came
from a very conservative background, comments on
the garb:

*I believe it served a good purpose in its day.
When the church tried to make it scriptural
and a requirement for membership, we often
failed to keep the deeper concern for individuals alive. When the mark of identification for
men drifted into a special garb for deacons and
ministers and became a clerical garb, we vio-
lated the principles of no hierarchy in religion.
The dress tended to portray hierarchy.*

A balanced evaluation comes from Kenneth Shaffer, a recent seminary graduate now serving as a librarian:

> I view the wearing of a prescribed garb and austere living both positively and negatively. It is positive in that it preserved identity and unity among the Brethren as well as serving to remind them that a Christian is to be in the world but not of the world. On the negative side, it destroyed personal and communal growth and creativity. It may be naïve to believe it is possible to preserve identity and unity while remaining open to the new, but I sincerely hope it is possible.

And Harold S. Martin, a teacher-minister who wears the special garb today, makes this comment:

> The wearing of the garb and practicing the principle of simplicity and uniformity and nonconformity help keep one from the burden and expense and waste of trying to keep up with the constantly changing fashions.

Continued agitation was produced in the church as the more conservative members sought to hold on to the garb to maintain simplicity and unity on the one hand, and on the other many members in cities and attending colleges and universities desired to see the regulations relaxed to permit personal freedom. This polarity, led to an exhaustive and soul-searching study of the whole question from 1909 to 1911. The monumental decision in 1911, at the end of two years of study, adopted by a very substantial vote of Conference, was the last important consideration of the whole issue by the Conference. It is of sufficient importance to show the changing thought of the Brethren, that it justifies printing here in full:

> Pursuant to the foregoing instructions "To

take the whole matter under advisement and to make a restatement" we proceeded as follows:

I. We examined prayerfully the scriptural grounds of Christian attire and found that Jesus and the apostles taught honesty and simplicity of life and modesty in dress and manners.

The scriptures bearing on the subject of dress and adornment are of several classes:

First. Jesus condemned anxious thought for raiment (Matt. 6:25-33; Luke 12:22-31).

Second. The direct teachings, such as 1 Tim. 2:9, 10; 1 Peter 3:3-5.

Third. Teachings on nonconformity to the world in general and that apply to dress on general principles, such as Rom. 12:1, 2; 1 Cor. 10:31; 1 Peter 1:14, 15; John 2:15-17.

II. Investigation shows that the early church fathers and our own church fathers taught strongly and uniformly against pride and superfluity in dress, and constantly in favor of gospel plainness.

III. The Minutes of Conference show that the Church of the Brethren has, throughout her history, stood firmly against the fashions of the age, and extravagance in all manner of living, and on the other hand has taught faithfully the principles of simplicity of life and personal appearance. And, furthermore the Conference has, from time to time, adopted means and methods with the view of maintaining gospel simplicity in dress in the church body.

Now, since the gospel teaches plain and modest dress and since this is taught in the form of an obligation, without rules and methods of application further than to exclude plaiting of hair, the wearing of gold, pearls and costly raiment, and believing that a form that agrees with the spirit of the teaching is helpful in maintaining the principles of plainness and simplicity in dress and adornment in the general church body, "it seemed good to us" to submit the following restatement:

1. That the brethren wear plain clothing. That the coat with the standing collar be worn, especially by the ministers and deacons.

2. That the brethren wear their hair and beard in a plain and sanitary manner. That the mustache alone is forbidden.

3. That the sisters attire themselves in plainly made garments, free from ornaments and unnecessary appendages. That plain bonnets and hoods be the headdress, and the hair be worn in becoming Christian manner.

4. That the veil be worn in time of prayer and prophesying (1 Cor. 11:1-16, RV). The plain cap is regarded as meeting the requirements of scriptural teaching on the subject.

5. That gold for ornament and jewelry of all kinds shall not be worn.

6. That no brother be installed into office as minister or deacon who will not pledge himself to observe and teach the order of dress.

7. That no brother or sister serve as delegate to District or Annual Meeting, nor be appointed on committees to enforce discipline, who does not observe the order of dress.

8. That it be the duty of the official body of the church to teach faithfully and intelligently the simple, Christian life in dress; and bishops, who are the shepherds of the churches, are required to teach and to see that the simple life in general is taught and observed in their respective charges.

9. That those who do not fully conform to the methods herein set forth, but who manifest no inclination to follow the unbecoming fashions, and whose life and conduct is becoming a follower of Christ, be dealt with in love and forbearance; and that every effort be made to save all to the church until they see the beauty of making a larger sacrifice for Christ and the church. But if, after every effort has been made, they, in an arbitrary spirit, refuse to conform to said methods, and follow the foolish fashions of the world, they may be dealt with as disorderly members: and in dealing with such cases, both the salvation of soul and the purity of the church should be kept in view.

10. That all are urged and implored, in the bonds of brotherly love and Christian fellowship, to teach and exemplify the order of the church in dress as a suitable expression of "the hidden man of the heart, in the incorruptible apparel of a meek and quiet spirit, which is in the sight of God of great price."

11. That upon the final adopting of this report it shall supersede all else in the Minutes on the subject of dress. (92:5)

Attempts to have this decision reconsidered were made in 1915. A few slight changes and clarifications were made at that time and the decision was reaffirmed in 1917. Since that time, although there have been resolutions of Conference affirming the values of the simple life, there has been no further attempt to legislate a form of garb for members of the church.

The trend in the Church of the Brethren after the

1911 "dress decision" was away from legislation and toward education and positive teaching on the values of simple living and modest dress for Brethren. For several years a "dress reform committee" appointed by the Annual Conference was active in the preparation of articles and tracts advocating modest and plain dress, and providing speakers for the promotion of this emphasis in district and Annual Conferences. Dr. Rupel summarizes where the Church of the Brethren stood in 1970 on this issue, as follows:

> *The situation of the church membership in 1970 regarding the wearing of the prescribed dress was analyzed as follows: A few members were wearing "plain dress," the style subsequent to the changes wrought with the passage of time; a somewhat plain dress, such as a cap for the sister and the absence of a necktie for a brother; and the majority of members were wearing no item of clothing identifying membership in the church, having adopted the fashionable attire of their socio-economic class.*
>
> *The mode of dress worn by the members of the Church of the Brethren was a unique product of their religious beliefs and cultural setting in America during the 19th Century. It represented a people living on the frontier, seeking a livelihood from the soil, and isolated from the luxury of imports and the influence of fashionable dress. A period of time was required to synthesize a mode of dress which identified the wearer as a member of this socio-religious group. The distinctiveness of the dress was dependent upon the extent of the interaction by group members with the larger society. The mode of dress became a visible symbol of the religious beliefs held by the group, or*

rejected by it. As the life-style of the Brethren became an ideal, this particular mode of dress was considered as ideal. Once the mode of dress was synthesized, there were objections to changes in the items or exchanges for other items.

As the tide of change and acceptance of the dress and other cultural accoutrements of society in general accelerated, many Brethren argued eloquently that the peculiarity of God's people was to be in manner of life and zeal for mission and educational endeavor, and that these weightier matters were not at all dependent upon a form of dress. Some leaders of the church saw its mission as the transformation of society and saw outward nonconformity as a barrier to the efforts of the church. Thus many became not only indifferent to such symbols of nonconformity as a special garb or the prayer covering but became actively hostile to them. The Brethren were caught up completely in urban culture and the increasing dependence upon technology.

Annual Conference spent a great deal of time discussing and legislating on many issues concerning the simple life during the 19th Century and the earlier years of this century. The emphasis upon gospel simplicity passed into an emphasis upon uniformity, legislated with strict sanctions.

A statement which summarizes the position of the early Church of the Brethren on simplicity of life was included in the address by Desmond W. Bittinger, to the Central Committee of the World Council of Churches, at Nyborg, Denmark, on August 22, 1958:

The Brethren accepted the Lordship of Christ as a cardinal tenet of their faith. They looked to him as their leader and Savior . . . The

Lordship of Christ implied for them absolute obedience to him who was to them the master of every life and of all life. . . . The Brethren were not ascetic. They did, however, develop a doctrine of nonworldliness and accepted disciplines austere and removed from the immediate ends of life. The Brethren were less involved in the physical comforts and the accumulation of wealth than they were in the deeper meanings and the final fulfillment of life.

Annual Conference several times ruled on the question of Brethren houses. Typical is Article 10, 1846:

About pride, in its various forms, which is creeping into the church, it is thought highly necessary that the Yearly Meeting instruct and urge it upon all the overseers of the churches to see especially to that matter, and protest strongly against all manner of superfluity and vanity, such as building fine houses, and having paintings, carpetings, and costly furniture, etc., together with adorning the body too much after the fashion of the world. We believe that we should deny ourselves, and abstain from these things, especially our laborers in the Word, who are called to be examples of the flock.

Even the use of lightning rods was frowned upon by the Conference, in Article 7, 1851:

Should Brethren have the privilege to put up lightning rods? Considered that we should not advise Brethren to do so, nor would we say to those who have them to take them down; but advise all our dear brethren to bear with each other in such matters and try to put their chief trust in God.

The Brethren style of life was reflected in the architecture and furnishings of their meetinghouses. After the turn of the century, however, the congregations began to build finer buildings, often in the style of church buildings of other denominations. Annual Conference spoke often during the 19th Century about trends. A brief minute in 1855, Article 14, states:

> *Is it conforming to the world to build meetinghouses? Answer: No, if built without unnecessary ornaments and only for the worship and service of God.*

The question of using musical instruments in Brethren meetinghouses agitated the church from time to time. In 1890 there was a brusque decision, Article 9:

> *Is it right for churches of the Brethren to use organs in their meetinghouses in worship? If not, what shall be done with those congregations who have them? Answer: No, and those who have them to be instructed to put them away, and if they will not, to be considered and dealt with as disobedient members.*

Later, Conference softened the stand to permit the use of instruments where it would not cause dissension in the congregation. The use of musical instruments now is almost universal in our churches.

In early meetinghouses, the use of a pulpit or platform for the preacher was not considered right.

Was there anything in the earlier meetinghouse which we have lost to our detriment? Anna M. Warstler, long-time worker in the church, comments:

> *The very simplicity of the structure bears the marks of the simple life: fellowship which begets intergenerational contacts and sharing.*

The meetinghouse also suggests coming together after having been out. It says clearly to me: gathering for renewal, group sharing in a family with a common goal, exploring together the deeper meanings of scripture. The meetinghouse idea would encourage smaller congregations which could mean a wider participation in decision-making on the needs of the group.

Allen C. Deeter, Manchester College professor, relates:

The Brethren meetinghouse had the advantage of a much more face-to-face and informal atmosphere than many of our present churches. I am delighted with the fact that many of our churches are introducing opportunities for sharing and witnessing by laymen, both in the leadership of worship and in the open times for sharing faith and concern.

Buildings which are built in a semicircle or in semifacing situations seem to me to be much better suited to our historic concern for community of faith than do the altar-centered or pulpit-centered, straight-facing, long, narrow church structures. Thus I would see a round or nearly square church more on the meetinghouse pattern as more in keeping with our community.

And retired missionary Mabel W. Moomaw suggests:

Less expensive structures should be built as places for fellowship and worship. Take a second look at our costly church kitchens. Elders Satvedi and Bhagat [Indian church leaders], at the close of their American tours told us, "It would appear that your church kitchen is the most important room of the church!"

There is also a growing concern about the design and cost of our buildings for worship and other functions of the church, particularly among the young people. Perhaps it is high time for an architect to do some creative study of how a church's ideals may be better translated into its architecture.

The Brethren concern for simplicity of life found expression for a time in concern about higher education. Some Brethren writers have declared that for a hundred years or so the Brethren were opposed to education. Perhaps a fairer evaluation would recognize the great zeal of the Brethren for home training of their children and their nurture by the church. The beginning of ferment for Brethren-led schools for secondary and higher education did lead to some interesting Annual Conference cautions, Article 12, 1852:

> *How is it considered by the Brethren, if Brethren aid and assist in building great houses for high schools and send their children to the same? Considered that Brethren should be very cautious and not mind high things, but condescend to men of low estate. Romans 12:16.*

As the pressure increased for Conference sanction, legislation changed in character. Schools and colleges were started and Conference sought to have them controlled by conservative Brethren and to have them run in strict conformity to Brethren ideals.

But the dikes would not hold. The Brethren, instead of retreating into a sectarian shell, drifted or else deliberately plunged into the main stream of American culture and life. Was there really a choice? The change seemed irresistible. Brethren youth eagerly sought higher education and went into such service professions as teaching in ever in-

creasing numbers. The Brethren moved to town
and changed inexorably from a rural folk to people
identified with the vast majority of Americans in
the cities, the suburbs, and the countyseat towns.
Today, the Brethren are almost indistinguishable
from their neighbors in habitat, dress, and adapta-
tion of their life-style to their cultural milieu.

Yet the Brethren are not totally comfortable in
this new world. There is a lingering, and now growing nostalgia for the simpler, quieter, less complex
and harried life which they believe their grandparents enjoyed. They are uncomfortably aware of
the technological juggernaut which has overrun
their life. Many do not believe they can or should
adjust to the rat race which modern urban life
seems to have become. So they persistently seek for
a life-style which is not a retreat but a genuinely
Christian response to the new age.

Someone wittily expressed the transformation
of Brethren life in this way: "The Dunker elder
bought an automobile and stepped on the gas; out
of the window went his broad-brimmed hat, followed by his wife's bonnet, followed by his whisk-
ers!"

Certainly the Brethren have learned much from
this pilgrimage through outward nonconformity to
the world. They have learned that rigid forms and
legalistic prohibitions do not achieve the kind of
spirit which must be characteristic of the obedient
follower of Christ. And that positive teaching of a
Christian life-style is more effective than stern
pronouncements of anathema on those who do not
outwardly conform. Again the Brethren are searching the scriptures for a truly Christian norm, a
basis for personal ethical decisions and a pattern
for church life which will encourage, nurture, and

demonstrate a personal and corporate life which is perfect freedom in perfect obedience to the Lord of the church.

Chapter 5

THE FAMILY OUR SANCTUARY

THE SIMPLE LIFE begins with the home and family. From the time the Brethren first settled in America, they were for the most part a rural people. Families were usually large and their whole life and work was based on the land. Following the example of the first leaders of the church, Alexander Mack and his colleagues, they sought to order their lives by the plain teachings of the New Testament, in simple holy obedience to the Lord, Jesus Christ. They tried to order their personal, family and church life by the patterns they found in New Testament accounts of the life of the early Christians. They developed a close-knit community of faith.

The family life of the Brethren was strong, stable and patriarchal. There was little opportunity for formal schooling. As we have seen, the Brethren attitude toward higher education for more than a century was one of apathy or active distrust. Nevertheless, the role of the family and the church in training children was crucial.

Outside of the family, the one center of Brethren life was the church congregation. Most Brethren congregations were made up of a solid nucleus of Brethren families, with a sprinkling of convinced individuals from other neighboring families. The leaders of the local congregations were the elders and deacons who were chosen from and by the congregation. The growth of the church came about through the conservation of the large families of children, most of whom stayed in the church and who, upon marriage, brought their spouses into the church if they were not already Brethren.

Although there are serious problems in maintaining stable family life in our time, there is both faith and evidence that the family unit made up of husband, wife, and children, will not only endure but prevail. The basic monogamous family unit is successful, biblical, and sociologically and psychologically sound. To be sure, there are wide variations in it. Some families have one or two children, some have eleven, some have none. In some the basic unit might be augmented by the presence of perhaps grandparents or a resident aunt. Some have only one parent. Some units consist of one lone person. Some are rich, some poor, many in the middle. Some are serene and comfortable; some full of unresolved tensions, even to the breaking point. Some families consciously plan their life; some drift with the tides.

We face some hard questions as we relate our concern for simple, uncluttered living to home and family. In earlier days, large families were common and children were an economic asset. The average Brethren family had eight or ten children. Now producing and rearing a child is a very costly process. The threat of overpopulation raises the question of family limitation. All young couples must decide how big a family to have. The human race has been fruitful and has multiplied and filled Earth. Because being parents is no longer considered an inalienable right but a privilege, simple living may well involve a resolution on the part of a married couple to have not more than two children, or perhaps to completely deny themselves parenthood by birth and adopt children instead. Good total stewardship of life may well mean zero population growth, and thoughtful Christians might well make family limitation a part of their obedience to God.

Garrett Hardin has written on this problem in *Society and Environment: The Coming Collision:*

> The right to breed implies ownership of children. This concept is no longer tenable. Society pays an ever larger share of the cost of raising and educating children. If parenthood is a right, population control is impossible. If parenthood is only a privilege, and if parents see themselves as trustees of the germ plasm and guardians of the rights of future generations, then there is hope for mankind.

The home is the place where the family lives. It can look like a fortress or a warehouse where the family retreats from a hostile world, surrounded by the spoils of greedy forays into the marketplace and the costly trappings of conspicuous consumption. Or it can be a place of beauty and hospitality, a place where the family sustains and renews its life and shares life with its neighbors. A Quaker query helps to give perspective to our home life: "Are you endeavoring to make your home a place of friendliness, refreshment and peace, where God becomes more real to all who dwell there and to those who visit it?"

How can we maintain true simplicity and yet have our homes comfortable and efficient? How can we avoid conspicuous consumption? How can we keep from what Brethren pioneer, Dan West, called "nest worship"? Can we buy or rent houses which are so costly that we must anxiously deny ourselves opportunities for culture sharing over a period of thirty years to pay for it? Should we have our houses so squeaky clean and polished that our children may not romp in them? Or houses that become museums more than homes? The simple life does not mean that we cannot have carpets on the floor or lace curtains at the windows that Conference legislation long ago proscribed. But it does mean that we can furnish our houses modestly and tastefully. Happy the home where the husband has the hobby of making good furniture and where everything purchased is for living rather than for mere display.

Elise Boulding, a sociology teacher and project director of the Institute of Behavioral Science at the University of Colorado, had a perceptive article in *The Christian Ministry* which dealt with the woman's role in planning the household:

> *What will the family look like in Zion, when no one will any longer "hurt or destroy in all my holy mountain"? Housing will be simpler than it is now, with more shared facilities between households. Since women and men will be partners in service to the community of Zion, they will do as the first Christians did, as the 17th-century Quakers did, and as other Christian groups from time to time have done who saw that women and men were alike gifted to serve the community in many ways. They will share the care of the children and the work of the home, each taking a turn at full care if the other must be abroad. . . .*
>
> *The interiors of our homes in Zion and the tools we use in them will be different, simpler, and less motorized. The tools we do use will liberate women for more meaningful activities than simply creating more elaborate setting for family living. . . .*
>
> *Frugality is one of the most beautiful and joyful words in the English language, and yet it is one that we are culturally cut off from un-*

*derstanding and enjoying. The consumption
society has made us feel that happiness lies in
having things and has failed to teach us the
happiness of not having things. Voluntary poverty movements have cropped up again and
again in human history, and their appearance
again today has a special meaning for women,
for all people that live in involuntary poverty,
and for the future of all of us as stewards of
our planet.*

Professor Boulding further points out that we
have trained our little girls to be consumer queens,
and little boys to be breadwinners who could support the consumer queens.

The Christian family which intends to be a caring, sharing group should also intend to be a good
steward of all the resources it uses in a genuinely
human and Christian style of living. The family
ought to choose the size and style of house, furniture, as well as all its activities and purchases, in
Christian frugality and after a study of its priorities. The world is in an energy crisis. In this situation, what shall the Christian family do? Can we
get along with fewer gadgets, simpler appliances? If
we have superfluous appliances, what shall we do
with them? Children now are aware of the need for
the conservation of energy. They go about turning
off lights and heat, when before they could not be
motivated by all the loud parental prodding we
could muster.

In *The Intentional Family*,* Jo Carr and Imogene
Sorley write:

*An overdose of gadgets can be depressing. Too
many gewgaws on the coffee table, too many
things hanging on the wall, are still clutter, no*

*From *The Intentional Family* by Jo Carr and Imogene
Sorley. Copyright 1971 by Abingdon Press.

matter how beautiful each piece may be. A museum is an interesting place to visit, but a frustrating place in which to live. Why not alternate what is out on the coffee table, enjoying each item in turn by according it a place of honor all its own?

My friend wailed, "What I really need is more cabinet space." Her more efficient neighbor countered, "No, what you really need is this much cabinet space, maybe less—and a whole lot less junk. You cannot operate effectively with so many things. Decide what you really need in order to get the task done and then get rid of the rest!"

We have a word for it—"impedimenta." We got it from the conquering army of the old Roman Empire which tagged its accumulation of personal baggage "impedimenta." And they considered it a real impediment, a distinct encumbrance. They much preferred to travel light.

It is still true. When we are too heavily burdened with things we are not really free to travel—whatever kind of traveling we have in mind. There is a very real sense of lightness and freedom that happens when we clean out the hall closet and throw away all the junk.

The Christian family can simplify its life by working together. This is far more difficult than it was when the whole family was needed to do the farm, garden, or household chores. But the "intentional" family can find ways in which tasks may be shared. Most fathers are sharing more now in the care of their children and are proud of their household skills. In this writer's home, we have come to a delightful division of labor. Since I no longer have pastoral responsibilities and my wife Mary is a schoolteacher, I have found great joy in learning to cook and in doing the laundry. I am honestly finding as much satisfaction in making a casserole and baking a crusty loaf of bread or ironing my wife's school dresses as I do in preparing a sermon or writing a chapter of this book!

Children who grow up without having a share in home tasks are underprivileged indeed. My son complained that all we ever asked him to do was to carry out the garbage. It takes thought and planning to provide opportunities for wholesome and enjoyable work for all, but it can be done. A boy can get great satisfaction out of learning to bake rolls, preparing a good omelet and patching his own Levis. And a girl can enjoy planting, caring for, and harvesting a small garden, or learning carpenter skills. These are not usually economic necessities, but they have great worth in teaching values.

Simple living, further, requires us to scrutinize our family's use of leisure time. Do our times of leisure draw the family together or fragment it? Is it really good stewardship of family living to let our children be run ragged by football, little league baseball, ballet lessons, activities of all kinds? Many of these no doubt are excellent. But where do we draw the line? Are all these involvements truly character building? Do they require too much time away from home? Are they too costly? Are any of them merely ways to get the children out of our hair and into the hands of educated "babysitters"?

There are many activities which provide good family fun. We will discuss the values of outdoor recreation later. But most of these activities provide for family participation. Time in camping, backpacking, fishing, canoeing, or church family camps can be richly spent. The family needs to provide for fun times at home also. Carr and Sorley, in *The Intentional Family*,* have some excellent suggestions for family fun:

> *Time for fun should be part of family living. And it should be jealously preserved. The attitude of levity is extremely important to the psychological health of the family.*

> *Fun has many facets. Some families go camping. Some families play tennis. Some build stereo sets, or keep bees, or watch stars, or hunt rocks, or hike in the woods. These are worthy pursuits and part of the growth of people.*

> *But fun is little ways, too. Did you know that one penny piece of bubble gum, having been sufficiently masticated, can be stretched a full city block?*

> *Fun is the permission of the attitude of levity. It happens only when people are relaxed. The person who is trying too hard to be intentional can move in a fog of serious contemplation that dampens the spirits of those around him. Walking around under a cloud of black worry and borrowed trouble like Joe Bftsplk merely increases the problems. It contributes nothing to their solution, and at the same time robs us of today. Better to do our homework; better to set aside a think-time. Then in uninterrupted concentration we can take out the problems, look at them square in the face, decide what possible solutions are available, and make the necessary moves.*

> *Having done that, we are free to enjoy this movement—free to see and enjoy our children,*

---

*From *The Intentional Family* by Jo Carr and Imogene Sorley. Copyright 1971 by Abingdon Press.

*to listen to their laughter, and to add to it
some of our own.*

The family should invest in creative games and
toys and in the materials for arts and crafts.

Worship is one of the family's most important
functions and one which unifies and enriches its
life. More than any other activity it centers family
life on that which is most important. If we are com-
mitted to the simple life as the seeking first of
God's Kingdom, there is nothing more appropriate
and significant for the family than worship. All
through their history Brethren have held the family
to be the church's basic unit. If it is, then the family's worship function is as important as the congregation's worship function in the larger community
of faith. Worship in the family can be a joyous, creative celebration of all that the family holds dear
and important; it can be a part of the total family
life which gives direction, tone, and inspiration for
all the other functions of family life.

Many of us can recall with deep satisfaction the
times of family worship in our childhood homes;
the reverent reading of the Bible, the earnest
prayers, the hymns and spirituals, the grace at
meals, the special times when family prayer became
a powerful, sustaining, unifying, inspiring peak in
the family experience. Today's crowded schedules
make it increasingly difficult to have the family together for worship; but it is not impossible. Many
families are finding creative ways to worship together. Each family must work out its own pattern
and seek those guides and resources which will
enrich and enable worship times which are memor-
able and celebrative.

Simplicity of family life means attention to all
our needs and wants. Ironically, the simplicity of
the early Brethren was sometimes only a matter of

garb and church architecture—they often lived in great affluence at the table. Today's Christian family, so far as it is possible, should choose wholesome food which is adequate for the family's nutritional needs, without waste or gluttony. When so many in the human family have no bread, Christians should look seriously at their appetites for cake and candy. To be sure, there are health-food fads and fancies which complicate our food habits rather than simplify them. But there is a growing popularity of home baking, rejecting the "petrified soapsuds" which much commercially produced bread has become. Homemakers are rediscovering the joy of home canning and freezing. The growing awareness of chemical additives and preservatives which are of dubious value and may even be dangerous to health has led to a simpler table and to better health.

The historic Brethren position on temperance, advocating moderation in all things which are good, and total abstinence from all that are harmful, is a sound one. There is no justification in the genuinely simple life for the use of liquor or tobacco. There is ample medical and scientific evidence of the harm they do to justify total abstinence from them, aside from the moral implications. The simple life has no need of the false serenity achieved from drugs, whether the hard, addictive ones which have become so grave a danger to our society, or the sedatives, stimulants or tonics which are wolfed down in tank-car loads by the American public.

The family living the simple life will also look at soft drinks. Are the drinks so lavishly advertised good for our bodies? Do they cause our children to have better teeth, better digestion? Would we not be better off using pure fruit juices?

Previously, we said that at one time the Brethren

made a great issue of the garb worn by the Brethren. Whatever values there may have once been in a prescribed garb which set the Brethren apart from their neighbors, we have long since done away with it as legalistic, and are convinced that it could not achieve in our time the values which it was supposed to safeguard. Nevertheless, there is a basic principle of simplicity which we should maintain in the wearing of clothing. The world of fashion can lead to slavery to the latest thing out, and often makes a mockery of modesty, simplicity, and even of beauty. Swift and radical changes of style in clothing usually are planned to make present styles quickly obsolescent, and to enhance sales. Some designers seem to try to outdo themselves in creating bizarre and often outrageously ugly garments. Simple living in our times will mean frugality in purchasing clothing, good taste, modesty, the use of materials which wear well, passing garments on from one child to another, the delight of home sewing. It may mean a real rebellion against the dictators of fashion.

What about the family car? How many Christian families need two or three cars? Now we know that the automobile is not only the major villain in air pollution, but that it is consuming irreplaceable fossil fuels at an alarming rate. It is also a juggernaut which has overrun civilization. We should reject the huge powerful machines which use enormous amounts of fuel in favor of smaller, more economical cars. We ought to resist buying a second car unless the need is absolute. We can use car pools, public transportation, bicycles, and the legs God has given us. (Bicycles need not be the ten-speed variety, but simpler machines.) The energy crisis, the pollution of the air, and Christian concern for our own and our neighbor's welfare are bringing about a revolution in our attitudes toward the automobile. The day of bigness, of building every year bigger, fancier and more powerful and faster automobiles is over. The huge automobile manufacturers are beginning to see this. Will the families who are building a life-style of uncluttered simplicity lead the revolution?

And finally, the home should be the family's refuge from storm and strain, the haven from the tensions, temptations and turmoil of the mad, whirling world. The home can be the center for serene, gracious, loving, caring family life which equips all the family members to live lives of goodwill, integrity, creative citizenship and compassionate service out in the world. But the home must be more than a mere service station, a place to refuel and to sleep after midnight. The Christian family ought to be an "intentional" family in which all the ideals and graces of a truly Christian life-style are fostered and successfully lived and taught.

Chapter 6

THE BIBLICAL PERSPECTIVE

WERE THE PLAIN Brethren only baptizing the economic and social necessity of simple living into a Christian virtue and then seeking a biblical rationale for it? That would probably be too simple an explanation. Throughout their history, Brethren have sought to know and to be guided by the mind of Christ as revealed in the Bible, particularly the New Testament. They have done this usually without falling into the trap of bibliolatry. At times, however, Brethren interpretations of Scripture have been strained or literalistic. Annual Conference decisions were based upon current understanding of biblical truths. The basic principle of honestly trying to find the will of God for personal and corporate living by reverent and open-minded study of the Word remains a sound and viable course today.

In this chapter we will examine several relevant scriptures which may give us valuable perspective for developing a life-style which embraces Christian simplicity. On the one hand the Bible teaches a way of life which presents a stern challenge to the materialism, greed, waste, and conspicuous consumption so characteristic of our modern culture. On the other hand, the Bible teaches a harmony between man and his neighbor, which would dispel his enslavement to clutter and his frantic pursuit of more and more material goods.

The church and the Christian person can make some impact only as the challenge is supported by and based upon biblical teachings which views the worth of man in vastly different terms.

Old Testament Teachings

The most important aspect of Old Testament teaching for our purposes is the story of creation. Let us begin with the biblical account as given in Genesis 1-3. Over against the widely prevalent idea that matter is inherently evil, the biblical story makes clear that the whole universe was created by God for his own good purposes and that when he looked upon his handiwork, he found it good, indeed, very good. This being so, we have no reason to consider it an enemy to the development of the spirit. Simple living then does not deny the value of things but puts them in their proper place, to be enjoyed, not rejected or wasted. Earth is holy because God made it for his purposes, chiefly as the home and the sustaining base for his highest creation, we who are created in his own image.

The Hebrew people never quite lost this concept that Earth is the Lord's, because he made it, and uses it for the working out of his purposes for us. The psalms are full of references to Earth as God's possession, and wonder at its beauty and its revelation of the creator's nature and will. Some of the most fruitful passages in the psalms for our study in understanding our relation to God's world are: Psalm 8:6-9; 19:1, 24:1,2, 65:9-13, the entire 104th psalm, and 147:7-11.

Certainly one of the loveliest hymns of praise to be found in any devotional literature is Psalm 65:9-13. It is a paean of praise for God's goodness in touching Earth in springtime with sunshine and rain, the miracle of seedtime. The picture of the green mantle of growing grain ripening into a golden har-

vest, as snowy flocks of sheep and goats dot the
pastures, is one of surpassing beauty. Such passages celebrate the wonder of our relationship to
the creator who has provided so bountifully and so
beautifully for his family. Since Earth and all its
bounty, the cattle on a thousand hills, the infinite
treasures of minerals and gems, the sparrow whose
fall is noted with deep compassion, the shadowy
creatures of the mysterious ocean deeps, and the
human family all belong to God, man must live in
reverent harmony with all creation, knowing that
we are but one part of the whole, and a "tenant of
the Almighty" rather than a lordly owner. What a
contrast to the attitude of the big stripmine opera-
tor who surveyed the vast rolling plains of eastern
Montana and cried, "It's not worth anything but
for the coal under it. Hell! Let's strip it!"

Unfortunately, many Christians have interpret-
ed the idea that we are given "dominion" over
Earth and all its creatures as license to kill, destroy, exploit, enslave, and waste. Note the relevant
passages in Genesis (NEB): "So God created man
in his own image. . . . God blessed them and said to
them, 'Be fruitful and increase, and fill the earth
and subdue it, rule over the fish in the sea, the birds
of heaven, and every living thing that moves upon
the earth'" (1:27,28). "The Lord God took the
man and put him in the Garden of Eden to till it
and care for it" (2:15). These two references come
from the two different major traditions regarding
the creation. But it is clearly not the intent of the
creator in either tradition that our supremacy in
the created order is a license to destroy. To have
dominion means to conserve, to use with reverence
and temperance, to manage for the good of the
whole creation. God gave us the privilege of using
creation for food, shelter and enjoyment. But pollu-

tion, waste, greed, selfish grabbing, wanton killing —these all deny the creator's purpose and upset the fine balance of nature which God has ordained.

Genesis 3:17-19 describes in poetic and powerful terms the curse put upon the good Earth by Adam and Eve's sin. It is not an arbitrary punishment. When we sin against our neighbor and God we are no longer in tune with Earth itself and the very ground suffers and becomes recalcitrant.

The Hebrew prophets show a keen insight into the relationship between our sin against our neighbor, our inhumanity, hatred, greed, and war, and the failure of crops and decimation of flocks and herds. Note the following passages:

> How long must the country lie parched and its green grass wither? No birds and beasts are left, because its people are so wicked, because they say, "God will not see what we are doing" (Jeremiah 12:4 NEB).

> Men sow wheat and reap thistles; they sift but get no grain. They are disappointed of their harvest because the anger of the Lord (Jeremiah 12:13 NEB).

Joel 1:10-12 tells of the utter desolation wrought by the terrible plague of locusts, the complete failure of the harvests, the destruction of all the fruit trees and vineyards. All of this, the prophet insists, has been brought about by the rebellion of Israel against the creator God, who has therefore sent or permitted the terrible army of locusts to come on their mission of devastation.

Hosea, most sensitive of prophetic figures, imagines a high court of justice in which God as both plaintiff and judge describes the inexorable consequences of sin for the creation:

> Hear the word of the Lord, O Israel; for the Lord has a charge to bring against the people

of the land: There is no good faith or mutual trust, no knowledge of God in the land, oaths are imposed and broken, they kill and rob; there is nothing but adultery and license, one deed of blood after another. Therefore the land shall be dried up, and all who live in it shall pine away, and with them the wild beasts and the birds of the air; even the fish shall be swept from the sea'" (Hosea 4:1-3 NEB).

Even in these portentous prophecies of devastation and famine, the prophets are reaffirming the unity of the creation. When man sins, it hurts not only his fellowman, but Earth itself. The apostle Paul reaffirms this indissoluble unity and its moral consequences in Romans 8:19-22.

THE NEW TESTAMENT TEACHINGS

This section will simply give suggestions for thorough study of the relevant passages in the New Testament regarding simple living and seek to draw some basic principles from them. (For an in-depth study of these passages and their message for our time, a stimulating guide is a book by Vernard Eller, Brethren professor at La Verne College, *The Simple Life.*)

First, let us look at the compendium of Jesus' teachings about the living in the Kingdom of God which is called the Sermon on the Mount. Kierkegaard explains Jesus' beatitude in Matthew 5:8, "Blessed are the pure in heart," by saying, "purity of heart is to will one thing." Central throughout the teachings of Jesus and consistently demonstrated in his life is this centering on one great priority, that of faithful obedience to God in his Kingdom. What then is the one thing which the follower of Christ wills? The key statement is in Matthew 6:33: "Set your mind on God's kingdom and his justice before everything else, and all the rest will come to you as well (NEB)." When we examine Jesus' constant teaching on the Kingdom of God, it is clear that he is not dealing with a geographic entity or a political domain. The Kingdom of God is the reign of God in human life. To seek first the Kingdom means to put obedience to the holy will of God in absolute supremacy in our lives. This is the "one thing" implied in purity of heart. Here is the ultimate biblical foundation for the simple life.

To seek his righteousness (AV) or justice (NEB) is a phrase well illuminated by the Hebrew word *shalom*. The word is often translated *peace;* but its meaning is far richer than that. It means righteousness, justice, compassion, mercy, God's ultimate will for good in the life of the persons upon whom he bestows his *shalom*. This was Jesus' gift to his disciples. He was the prince of *shalom*. "The kingdom of God is not eating and drinking, but justice, peace, and joy, inspired by the Holy Spirit" (Romans 14:17 NEB). When the ultimate priority in one's life is this Kingdom, this *shalom* of God, then things can no longer enslave one but become one's servants. Instead Jesus promises that whatever is really needful will be provided for us. Here is the secret of the uncluttered life. And many other teachings of Jesus reinforce this all-important truth.

Pastor Larry Fourman says:

The most important part of the simple life is religious. In its essence, simple living grows out of a commitment to God which is single. In Matthew 6, Jesus says to his disciples, "be concerned above everything else with his kingdom and what he requires, and he will provide you with all these other things." Having the Kingdom of God as our greatest con-

cern is the foundation source and inspiration for simple living. This means above all else trusting God to provide the basic necessities in life—food, shelter, clothing.

Earlier in Matthew 6, in his teaching on the light of the body, Jesus suggests to us the meaning of simple living. "If your eyes are clear, your whole body will be full of light; but if your eyes are bad, your body will be in darkness." What are clear eyes? The answer is suggested in Matthew 6:24: "You cannot serve God and money." Clear eyes are those focused entirely upon God. The Kingdom of God is their primary concern. Bad eyes are those focused both on God and the desire to obtain material security. These eyes are double-focused. Simple living grows out of a life-orientation which is focused on the Kingdom of God. This is a life which is increasingly uncluttered by the many distractions which keep the Kingdom from coming in its fullness.

The simple life-style which grows out of this commitment to Jesus as Lord and Savior is primarily life-affirming rather than life-negating. The Christian experiences in Jesus Christ God's "YES," his affirmation of life, all life. In this overwhelming experience of affirmation, of acceptance, one is led to live with a new singleness of purpose which Jesus clearly describes in the Beatitudes (Matthew 5:3-10).

H. Richard Niebuhr, in a thoughtful book on the church and its ministry, states that the ultimate purpose of the church is the increase of the love of God and neighbor. To put the Kingdom of God and his *shalom* first in one's personal life and in the life of the church, frees us from all lesser priorities so that we can single-mindedly pursue this goal.

The entire section of the Sermon on the Mount (Matthew 6:25-34, of which the summary is in verse 33) is a powerful and clear argument for simple living. There is in it no argument for a life-denying, narrowing asceticism. Jesus says that when we see all earthly goods in relation to the Kingdom of God, then we are freed from anxiety, from clutter, from obsession with getting, and are free for faith, joy, and justice.

Let us now examine other passages from the Gospels which support the great principles enunciated in the Sermon on the Mount. In Luke 10:1-12, we find the account of Jesus' sending out of seventy-two disciples to prepare the way for his later coming. They were to go uncluttered by "purse, pack, or extra shoes." As they went on mission they were to be content with the food and shelter offered them. Even Jesus himself said, "The Son of man has no place to lay his head." Missionaries, service workers, and Peace Corps workers have long since learned the wisdom of being free of too many possessions on their missions of healing and sharing. When Jesus sent out the twelve on their first two-by-two mission, their instructions for simplicity were even more explicit: "Provide no gold, silver, or copper to fill your purse, no pack for the road, no second coat, no shoes, no stick; the worker earns his keep" (Matthew 10:9,10 NEB).

In the story of Jesus' visit in the Bethany home of Mary and Martha (Luke 10:38-42) he gently and tactfully tells Martha not to fuss with too many things, too big a meal; Mary, sitting at his feet to listen, had chosen the better priority.

Jesus' confrontation with the rich young man (Luke 18:18-27) brings out his attitudes toward the ways in which great possessions can enslave. Loving the eager young man, Jesus bluntly told him that the one thing he must do is to sell everything he had and give to the poor; then he would have riches in heaven, and could become a follower of the Master. Was Jesus here saying that wealth is an absolute barrier to the Kingdom? Or was he saying that in this case, wealth had blinded and enslaved the man, and therefore he must make a clean break? Certainly he did not rule out wealthy persons from discipleship. But never must wealth of money or property be the *first* in one's life. It must become servant to the high purposes of the Kingdom of God. Could a rich man be saved? Yes, but it isn't easy.

The parable of the rich man and Lazarus (Luke 16:19-31) is most instructive. The rich man went to hell not because he was rich, but because his riches had made him insensitive to human need and suffering, even at his door. Lazarus was carried to Abraham's bosom not because he was poor, but because he had found shelter in the mercy of God in this life, even while spurned from Dives' door.

Still another of Luke's fine human interest parables is that of the rich man who built great new barns (Luke 12:16-21). Was Jesus saying that it is wrong to build large barns and warehouses in which to store the fruits of a bountiful harvest? No, this was not the man's sin. But his attitudes toward his great harvest condemned him. Instead of thinking of his corn and wine as a sacred stewardship, to be shared with his hungry brothers, he could only congratulate himself on his agricultural expertise and his prudence and sit back to enjoy it all selfishly. Jesus didn't even dignify his conduct by calling it sin; the man was a fool. Thus Jesus holds up to our gaze the sinful folly of a person, in any age, in any land, who selfishly amasses wealth and remains a pauper in the sight of God.

Two small gems of parables of the Kingdom of

God in Matthew 13:44-46 deal with the question of priorities and illuminate the teaching on giving the Kingdom first place in our lives, thus freeing us for that which brings eternal profit.

The powerful allegory of the sheep and the goats at the final judgment (Matthew 25:31-45) illuminates the question of our use of things and our attitude toward the needy. Here Jesus is saying that in the judgment, our fate ultimately rests upon our record of our use of God's gifts to us. Our worship will be tested by whether it has issued in service to the hungry, the thirsty, the naked, the sick, the prisoner. We are indeed saved by the infinite amazing grace of God as perfectly demonstrated and revealed in Christ the Lord. But whether we have lived by that grace will be seen in the extent to which we have used our lives and treasure in ministering to "the least of these, my brethren."

Can there be any shadow of doubt about the thrust of Jesus' teachings on things, money, possessions, and our use of them? He never counsels that we despise the world and its bounty, or that wealth is inherently evil. But when our lives are centered in the pursuit of the Kingdom of God and his *shalom*, then things take their proper place. All things become ours; there will be no room for anxiety, no troubled hoarding, no grasping for more, no depriving of our neighbor, no blind callousness to human hunger and need. The simple life is not one of a narrow, stingy asceticism, but one of freedom from greed and freedom for sharing love.

Groups of Christians who seek to return so far as possible to the pattern of primitive Christian living make much use of certain passages in the Book of Acts. Christian concern for the welfare of all members of the church is expressed with clarity in Acts 2:42-46 and 4:32-35. It seems clear that the

Jerusalem church experimented for a time with a form of communal living and sharing in which many who had property sold it and put the proceeds into the common treasury from which all might draw according to their needs. One of the spectacular abuses of the system is described in Acts 5:1-12, the story of Ananias and Sapphira, who sought to have the esteem of the church for such total commitment but withheld part of the sale price for their own secret use—and paid with their lives. We cannot know how universal the practice was even in this primitive church. Many Christian groups have tried and still try to follow this pattern literally.

The basic principle found in the Acts account is the complete commitment of things, wealth, and property to Christ and to the community of faith so that all the needs of the community are met. No members of the church considered their property their own, but held it in trust for the good of all. This basic principle may be universally valid, whether or not a church may adopt the total communal pattern for its life.

The apostle Paul comments upon several important aspects of a simple Christian life-style. He expresses at several points his concern that food and drink must never be a barrier to brotherhood, but we must often deny ourselves things that are in themselves good, for the sake of others in Christ (See Romans 14:15—15:3). He sums up his concern here in these compassionate words: "Each of us must consider his neighbour and think what is for his good and will build up the common life" (15:2 NEB).

In his own personal life, Paul came to a fine sense of propriety in relation to things (See especially Philippians 4:10-19). It is instructive to note his monumental effort to collect from the Gentile churches a large sum of money to relieve the suffering of the Judean Christians in a time of famine. Here in his teaching he stresses the use of wealth as an instrument of brotherly love and concern.

Perhaps Paul's most significant teaching here is found in 1 Corinthians 7:29-32 (NEB):

> *What I mean, my friends, is this. The time we live in will not last long. While it lasts, married men should be as if they had no wives; mourners should be as if they had nothing to grieve them, the joyful as if they did not rejoice; buyers must not count on keeping what they buy, nor those who use the world's wealth on using it to the full. For the whole frame of this world is passing away. I want you to be free from anxious care.*

Here Paul is reaffirming the great principle we found in the teaching of Jesus in Matthew 6:33, that the Kingdom of God must have absolute priority. Paul believed that the end of the age was at hand. In the light of the imminence of Christ's return, to be obsessed with the acquisition or use of things would be foolish. Some interpreters have said therefore that Paul was mistaken, that an ethic based upon his eschatological outlook is faulty or useless. But rather, it is of timeless value, for he is saying that though we may not know the date of Christ's return, Christians must always live in expectation and hope. They will always live so that whenever the end of the age may come, they are ready, and have a set of values built in the light of eternal perspectives.

In his book, *The Simple Life*, Vernard Eller has very helpful comments upon the validity of Paul's teaching:

> *What is essential . . . is to discover how Paul*

uses this eschatological expectancy, what role it plays in and what contribution it makes to his ethical formulation. It would seem, in the first place, that his expectancy does not change the content of the ethic, that is, it does not make anything right that otherwise would be wrong or make wrong what otherwise would be right. What it does do is sharpen and clarify priorities.

The biblical perspective on simple living is basically that the follower of Christ will seek first, give first place to the Kingdom of God and his *shalom*. Thus he will be able to judge the true worth of all material things and will be able to use them as instruments of love, and a genuine enrichment of life. He will see himself as a "tenant of the Almighty," living in and using the world God has created as a partner of God, rejoicing in the beauty, order and bounty of creation, and living as a faithful steward.

Chapter 7

THE CITY AND THE WILDERNESS

BRETHREN HAVE always been advocates of the "work ethic," a strong conviction that honest work and lots of it is not only necessary to sustain life, but that it is the most wholesome use of time. They found the apostle Paul's injunction in 2 Thessalonians 3:10-12 (NEB) as both congenial and mandatory. The essence of Paul's thought in this passage was, "the man who will not work shall not eat . . . To all such we give these orders, and we appeal to them in the name of the Lord Jesus Christ to work quietly for their living." They liked the idea of Christ as a laboring man, a carpenter who made stools and ox yokes of superlative design and strength. Children were taught early to share in the chores, and soon to take their place with adults as workers in field and kitchen. As Brethren families became urbanized opportunities for children and youth to share in creative family-centered work swiftly disappeared.

Today, the advance of urbanization, automation, and the increase of population with a greatly enlarged work force, have brought for most people a much shorter work week. Everyone faces the problem of wise and creative use of leisure time. To complicate the problem, there has been an enormous increase in opportunity for spectator sports, and myriad forms of commercialized recreation.

Some question the sharp division often made be-

tween work and leisure. Pastor Leland Wilson
writes:

> *The concern for finding more leisure time is
> self-defeating. It does not speak of the simple
> life in which one is living out his purpose in
> nonleisure time. Our need is not for loads of
> leisure; it is for discovering regular pursuits
> that are meaningful. Leisure is useful only for
> providing some rhythm to life—essential, but
> only as the space between words, the occasion-
> al rest in a piece of music. The whole emphasis
> upon leisure has been and necessarily is the
> preoccupation of the affluent.*

Some of us find ourselves in vocations so rewarding and so creative that the time of work and the
time of play are indistinguishable. Nevertheless, for
better or for worse, most of us find that we are
engaged in tasks which occupy only thirty to forty
hours of the week, and have large blocks of time to
spend in other ways. Our Christian stewardship is
just as important in relation to our time as it is to
our possessions or to the resources of good Earth.
We will need to find ways to use this bonanza of
time which enrich life and promote the Kingdom of
God.

The title of this chapter suggests the locus of the
two major aspects of our time expenditure. The city
stands for the locus of work, business, trade, commerce, residence, the earning of our daily bread.
The wilderness stands for the place of recreation,
the locus of those activities which renew our life in
play and enjoyment of the beauty of the created
world. Harvey Cox has pointed out man's need for
alternation of work and play, earning and spending,
exposure to the seething currents of business and
human striving, and solitude. This is not setting
the "evil, satanic city" over against an idyllic and

romantic "nature," but recognition of the values of both, and the health there is to be found in acceptance and full usage of both environments.

The Christian doctrine of creation makes us sensitive to wilderness in a new way. The pioneers, and this is true of Brethren pioneers, saw the wilderness—forest, prairies, desert and mountain as adversary, to be tamed, conquered, plowed, exploited. In our time we are seeing that we have gone too far in our conquest. We have so wasted and despoiled the land that there is not enough wilderness left for the needs of the human family for renewal. Good stewardship of Earth provides for a proper balance between wilderness and cultivation, between city and open country, so that there is room for man to breathe, to play, to find solitude and silence, and to affirm and sustain his kinship with the multitude of wild things which also claim Earth as their home. As John Muir put it, "In God's wilderness lies the hope of the world . . . The galling harness of civilization drops off, and the wounds heal ere we are aware." The motto of the Sierra Club which John Muir founded and which is a powerful force for conservation of wilderness and the vast resources of our country is, "In wilderness is the preservation of the world."

The Christian persons therefore who desire to live a life of uncluttered simplicity in obedience to God, do not run from the city as if it were totally evil. They see it as the place of their residence, their formal education, their daily work, their business and their commerce with others. But they also see the need for wilderness, and for living in a reverent, respectful creative relationship to it. There has been much fear expressed that the population explosion and the irreversible destruction of wilderness may lead to its total loss within a generation or two. But happily the worldwide concern for environment is taking effect. The creation of Shenandoah National Park in the Blue Ridge Mountains of Virginia, in an area where the hillsides and the valleys had been denuded and despoiled, has demonstrated that wilderness can be renewed. In less than forty years, the whole area has returned to a healthy and growing forest, with trees up to seventy feet tall, and a balanced population of all kinds of wild animals.

Speaking of the threat of overpopulation, Buckminster Fuller argues that the rapid industrialization of the developing countries will stabilize world population by 1985. It may be that God is already renewing Earth, even before we dreamed he could.

Let us examine some ways in which creative and Christian use of leisure time can affect our total life. As we have looked at the values of wilderness, we have seen how important it is that we conserve and enjoy it. Leopold, in *Sand County Almanac*, distinguishes between the persons who use wilderness only to collect trophies, to kill and destroy, and those who go to enjoy, learn, and recreate their own life:

> *The trophy recreationist has peculiarities that contribute in subtle ways to his own undoing. To enjoy he must possess, invade, appropriate. Hence the wilderness that he cannot personally see has no value to him. Hence the universal assumption that an unused hinterland is rendering no service to society. To those devoid of imagination, a blank place on the map is causeless waste; to others, the most valuable part. (Is my share of Alaska worthless to me because I shall never go there? Do I need a road to show me the Arctic prairies, the goose pas-*

tures of the Yukon, the Kodiak bear, the sheep meadows behind McKinley?)

It would appear, in short, that the rudimentary grades of outdoor recreation consume their resource-base; the higher grades, at least to a degree, create their own satisfactions with little or no attrition of land or life. Recreational development is a job not of building roads into lovely country, but of building receptivity into the still unlovely human mind.

Creative leisure makes for good physical and mental health. Those recreational activities which get us outdoors and provide wholesome exercise truly re-create. The average person spends many hours watching TV, most of which is a dreary wasteland. Television has an immense potential, but the industry has so totally commercialized it, and has so filled its screen with sex, violence, and propaganda, that the Christian family needs to be on guard that TV does not become a dangerous and debilitating substitute for good recreation. Television has also promoted spectatoritis instead of participation in outdoor sports. Enjoyable as it may be to watch football, baseball, basketball and the Olympics on TV, there is infinitely more recreational value in games with neighborhood kids, hiking, cycling, backpacking, and all the participation sports.

Creative leisure takes time, thought, and ingenuity, as contrasted with buying all the latest recreational gadgets. Glee Yoder's new book, *Take It From Here*, is chockful of creative ideas for family recreation. She teaches us how to use everyday materials and the inifinite treasure house of nature in creating things of beauty, or just to have fun with them together. Use of this book may help to get many of our families away from the insatiable and destructive need for manufactured toys. We should be selective in buying toys. All the apparatus of war, such as guns and soldiers, and dolls which give false impressions of growing up and exalt expensive wardrobes and accessories, must be seriously evaluated for how they influence children's values. Some families buy, for children of six or eight, motorized bikes and go-carts which are not only of questionable value in the child's growth, but are downright dangerous. A Christian family should be wary of purchasing playthings dictated by the vast commercial interests which wax fat on destructive "toys" which children beg their parents to buy.

The greatest expansion and change in the use of leisure time has come about in opportunity to travel. The automobile, the road systems which make distant scenic areas and recreational sites accessible in ever shorter travel time, have all greatly expanded leisure travel. But here, too, there are subtle dangers to the simple life. Many families come home from a vacation spent in frantic rushing to and fro, so tired that the vacation time has been worse than useless. Ken Shaffer writes of the human element in travel:

> *The best forms of recreation are those which help us to relate to our others in constructive ways. While realizing that we all need to be alone at times, the joy of fellowship with others can be sublime. Most of life is much more enjoyable when it is shared. Given such an understanding, travel is one of the best forms of entertainment, as contact with new people and ideas usually encourages both individual development and social ties.*

Many who were consulted in the preparation of this book listed travel as one of the most creative and family-centered of all leisure-time activities. Many of them point out the danger of losing the best values by too much use of mechanization—big cars, elaborate trailers and mobile homes, boats, motorbikes, dune buggies, and snowmobiles. Mechanization can so complicate leisure time and travel that the recreational values are lost, and the commercial interests which have enticed us to buy more and more expensive travel and recreational equipment have covered the simple life with a cloud of dust.

When asked about the best and worst forms of recreation and entertainment, Professor Kenneth Brown said:

> *Most conducive: Biking, camping (without making it a technological exhibition), boating (sans motors). Individual sports, noncompetitive team sports. Most inimical: Competitive spectator sports. Technology recreations (auto racing, snowmobiles). Whatever manifests power, coercion, competition, rather than harmony, unity, repose.*

Leon Neher sees modern technology as an ally of the simple life in the area of recreation:

> *I see modern technology as a possible tool for simple living, so long as it doesn't become an end in itself. Further automation of our farming operation will give us more free time. Granted, there is a point of diminishing returns at this point. Beware.*

Travel as a family can often serve many purposes. It can be not only recreational, but may also promote vocational interests. Vernard Eller writes of the combination of these values:

> *My busyness is serving the church. My effort is to take the family along and involve them in the busyness as much as possible. Rather than me doing it while they stay at home, we do it. I have lost the line between vacation and voca-*

tion. Theoretically I have three summer months off. Traveling to church camps, conferences, summer schools, etc., is vacation-vocation for me and pretty much vacation for the rest of the family. When what I most enjoy doing (preaching, teaching and writing) can also be a service to others, that is the best of all possible worlds—particularly when I can involve the family rather than leaving it. Most inimical forms of recreation: Those which produce nothing but individual momentary pleasure, and cost a great deal of money in the process.

As you plan for the best use of your family's leisure time and choose ways to have the most creative vacation, ask whether oversized campers, trailers, boats, and snowmobiles really make for good recreation, or are they costly and sometimes destructive of the environment? Do we buy them to have something bigger than our neighbors have? Recreational vehicles have become a great threat to the fragile environment in such places as the Mojave Desert, mountain wilderness areas and forests. Delicate ecosystems have been damaged in some places beyond repair by motorbikes, jeeps, and dune buggies. Waterways and lakes have been tragically polluted by motorboats whose owners have been careless about oil spills and garbage disposal. The pristine beauty and serenity of snowclad mountains and forests has been shattered by the unbearable noise and speed of snowmobiles.

We ought to explore the recreational and environmental values of hiking, bicycling, snowshoeing, and cross-country skiing, thus enhancing health, respecting the environment, reducing pollution, and saving money.

Leisure time can be creative. Glee Yoder's book

points to the many possible ways in which families —adults and children—can create articles of beauty and usefulness using common things. Hobbies can be the "pack rat" kind in which we collect vast quantities of useless things which have neither esthetic or utilitarian value; or hobbies can become delightful activities which enhance the beauty of our homes.

Creative leisure may mean development of artistic skills. Beginning with such illustrious persons as Dwight D. Eisenhower and Winston Churchill, many mature persons have discovered painting as a creative hobby, whether or not they ever sell a painting. While it can become a very expensive pursuit, many find photography to be creative and wholesome. I have found nature photography a most rewarding hobby. Some have found that making artistic and novel articles out of common things found in forest, desert and seashore has great fascination. Grace Hollinger, a former Church of the Brethren General Board staff person, has developed a creative hobby using weeds, seed pods, driftwood, bark, stones and other common natural objects to make beautiful decorative arrangements for home and office. The list of possibilities in this field is endless. Growing numbers of people have found great recreational and esthetic values in rock collecting. The search for fossils, geodes, crystals, and semiprecious stones which have intrinsic beauty or can be polished and shaped into articles of beauty and even commercial worth, is healthful and creative. Many of these kinds of recreational pursuits can be excellent family projects. They can be the focus of vacation trips and leisure-hour projects throughout the year.

Music as a family recreation need not be as professionally perfect as that produced by the Trapp family, or as famous and lucrative as that produced by some TV family personalities today. But making music together as a family can be among the very finest uses of leisure time. The TV and the stereo must not be permitted to take the place of music produced by individuals and families as creative leisure-time.

Such crafts as ceramics, woodworking, stitchery and needlecraft have traditionally had a large place in the Christian family, and have infinite possibilities in our time.

The use of leisure time in voluntary services is a growing area of interest. A Christian style of life sees the increased amount of time which is not needed for earning bread as a great opportunity for service. Many young people have found that the week-long or weekend work camp in which a group serves in some needy area becomes a creative kind of leisure-time recreational activity. For a number of years, groups of youth from several churches in Bakersfield, California, have spent the Easter holidays in such service as constructing a school building or a water system for impoverished Indians. Summer work camps of longer duration have been attractive to youth.

But such leisure voluntarism is of even greater potential worth to older persons. The increased amount of leisure time available to couples when their children have left home, or upon retirement, can be put to creative use. There are countless openings for a couple or an individual in short-term or long-term volunteer service. When large blocks of time are not available, many older persons can serve in local community action programs. Mature persons have found great delight and a new lease on life in being foster grandparents. Every local church ought to have a "director of volunteer services," who can control the leisure-time service activities of persons in the congregation who wish to give time, talents, skills, and love in serving projects in the community.

The simple life is not a barren life. It can be a rich, fruitful, full life, without becoming cluttered. Most of us will find ourselves throughout our lifespan with a great deal of time which is not required for the work which sustains life and which can be an outlet for our creativity. This time may be as creative as that spent in work. The Christian use of leisure time contributes to the well-being of ourselves, our families, and our neighbors. It will not be a wasting of strength and resources in spectatoritis, or in pursuits that destroy our fellow creatures in God's world. It is healthy and health-giving. It is characterized by the wholesome enjoyment of the creation, never in its despoiling or destroying.

And one further thought. Life should not be compartmentalized into three periods: education, work, and retirement. Rather, throughout life we should alternate among these three functions. Education is a continuing process. We can continue to experience formal and informal learning through old age. There can be periods of retirement—leisure—in every period of life. And even after the age when adults retire from wage-earning work, there can be many opportunities, so long as health permits, to do creative work, serving the community and the family, and creating things of value and beauty. All life should provide such alternation among work, learning, worship, and play, among the city, the sanctuary, and the wilderness.

Chapter 8

MONEY

WHAT IS MONEY? And what does it have to do with simple living? The plain fact is that money is simply a medium of exchange. By its use, we exchange our time and talents for the goods we need or want. The trilogy of time, talent and treasure isn't all that simple; time and talent are God-given, money is not and we must not pretend that it is.

We use interesting nicknames for treasure. Money is one. We call money "filthy lucre" when we want to show our contempt for it (a contempt which we exhibit most when we really want to hold tightly to it). Young people call it "bread"; they are more nearly right. We speak of earning our daily bread. We really get money for our work, then we spend it for bread—or a thousand other things. But the basic nature of bread makes it a good synonym for money.

We have often quoted wrongly: "Money is the root of all evil," while the Bible says, "The *love* of money is the root of all evil things . . ." (1 Timothy 6:10 NEB). Money is important. One of the basic tests of simple living as a Christian life-style is the manner in which the Christian earns, saves, invests, spends, hoards, or gives money. The excellent statement on the Theological Basis of Personal Ethics, adopted by the 1966 Church of the Brethren Annual Conference deals with the deep meaning of our use of money in these terms:

*Life and property are gifts to us from God. As
a living soul and by God's grace, we are ena-
bled to have dominion over the Earth and to
care for our neighbors. Separation from God
brings thorns and thistles, anxiety, sickness,
isolation, and death to man (Genesis 3). In
Jesus Christ we gain abundance of life, the
hope of resurrection, and the promise of a new
heaven and a new Earth. Life and property as-
sume their rightful significance when we recognize that we are to be a good steward of God's
gifts, using them in nourishment of and care
for our neighbor.*

We have often talked of stewardship and stewardship education in the church as if it had to do
with money alone. Sometimes the persons directing
stewardship campaigns in the churches stress tith-
ing as the ideal method of giving, but now the stewardship literature and appeals more often stress
the totality of life, and urge people to see all of
their time, talent, and possessions belonging to
God, and teach family financial planning from this
total stewardship basis. The thrust of our argument
throughout this book has been that as Christian
persons, we regard all of life and all our so-called
possessions as entrusted to us by the Lord, to be
used for the purposes of his Kingdom. Simple living
means good stewardship of all things.

H. Spenser Minnich, a long-time exponent of
good stewardship, uses a different term:

*I think of life as a trusteeship. What is a trust-
ee? A person in possession of that which he
does not own but has all the responsibilities of
an owner and who in due time closes his work
leaving his record as his report. Jesus gave us
his life as an example and sends us forth with a
mission of love. This is our trusteeship. We are*

given life, time, ability and substance as our operating assets.

God has given us an abundant world, and tremendous capacity to have dominion. Through Jesus and teaching examples of good stewards recorded in the Bible and elsewhere we learn the vital principles of living.

The Bible has much to say about money. An astonishing proportion of Jesus' teaching is about money, and the uses of it. On the meaning of money, we might start with a careful examination of these passages: Job 42:10-17; Psalm 37:25; Proverbs 22:1, 30:8, 9; Ecclesiastes 5:13; Matthew 6:19, 13:22, 19:16, 22:15; Luke 6:24; 1 Corinthians 4:12, 16:1-4; 1 Timothy 3:3, 6:10; Hebrews 13:5. One might find it very profitable to see how many of Jesus' parables deal with the use of money, or to study Paul's teaching about giving in his letters.

How have the Brethren regarded money? In earlier chapters we have noted their concern that the brothers and sisters should never spend money on vulgar display in their homes, or on dress and adornment of the person. Sometimes the frugality which was the natural outgrowth of the Brethren's sturdy German cultural heritage and rural environment led to baptized penuriousness. They have at times been guilty of greed and materialism, with a touch of Pharisaism about it. And there have been among them persons who have willfully moved into a proud and blind affluence. Should Brethren, or any Christians, become rich? If through accident of inheritance, or careful management of resources, they become affluent, what should be their attitude toward money?

Christians are compelled to apply the basic principles of simple living to the uses of their money. Each of us must examine for himself and his family what this means. Are there some ways of earning a living that must be ruled out? At least, we must scrutinize with great care areas of earning which depend upon the manufacture and distribution of things which are evil or destructive. Can we conscientiously engage in work which produces and distributes liquor, tobacco, or war materials?

What about making money through investments? In recent years, the Church of the Brethren has become sensitive about the investment holdings of its General Board and its church-related institutions. Because of this aroused conscience on investments, the Brethren have disposed of stocks and bonds which are connected with war industries and companies which perpetuate racial injustice in this country or abroad. But even here there is an honest difference of opinion. Should this church totally divest itself of such investments, or should it make its voice heard, as a stockholder, against the policies of the corporation? How effective would its protest be? How can investors most effectively influence the policies of business?

In the area of gambling and lotteries there is less controversy. May the Christian person get money in these ways? The Brethren paper on the theological basis of personal ethics has some pertinent counsel on this matter:

> *One of the most critical social problems of today is the widespread popularity of small lotteries and policy games, from which organized crime receives its major source of income. The hope to gain something for nothing is a flight from reality, so much so that for many persons gambling is habitual and uncontrollable. Life before God is not an unrealistic hope for a lucky break, but is a way of facing the future in the confidence that Jesus Christ dis-*

*closes God's steadfast love and care for hu-
mankind. The risks it runs are those of faith
undertaken in loving concern for one's fellowman and the surprises it expects are not those
of chance but the free operation of God's
grace. The spirit of Christ is that of charity,
sacrifice, and self-giving rather than that of
gaming in order to gain the property of the
neighbor, no matter how worthy the use to
which the gain is put. Christians are called to
act and speak openly against the sources of organized crime and to work for the release of
those who are so economically oppressed that
they are inclined to gamble. It must be recog-
nized that some prizes appeal primarily to recognition or enjoyment rather than to chance
gain. The Christians are to distinguish between gambling and innocent games in conversation with their fellow Christians.*

State lotteries have greatly enlarged the area of
temptation for many Christians. The states of Pennsylvania and Maryland, in which there are many
Brethren, are running state lotteries with vast and
persuasive advertising campaigns. The principles
enunciated in the ethics paper are fully relevant
here. However worthy the ends for which the
money is used, either by the state or by the "lucky"
winners, lotteries are still gambling, appealing to
the desire to get something for nothing. They are
basically evil because those who buy the tickets are
usually those who can least afford to lose the
money. Furthermore, the experience of other states
has shown that it is very difficult to keep them out
of the sticky fingers of the organized crime forces.
Betting on horse races and sports events is in the
same category.

The Christian person must decide also whether

such a transaction as speculation in grain futures, which has been the cause of wild fluctuations in the prices of farm products, is a Christian use of money. Christians are not immune from temptation to be unethical in the stock market and speculation.

The ethics paper summarizes some of the basic questions on one's relation to money and principles for making Christian decisions on them in this paragraph:

> *In an affluent society in which many persons are seeking security through possessions, it must be affirmed again and again that life does not consist of the abundance of things and that the good life is not found in material possessions. Christians must see affluence as either a potential blessing in the establishment of the Good Life among all persons and nations, or a possible peril greater than poverty. Luxurious living must not be allowed to crowd out involvement in social issues such as civil rights, poverty or urban decay, nor must materialism divorce us from the great issues of our day. In their search for security Christians are called to resist the many pressures of our materialistic living and to practice the "simple life" as God's faithful stewards of our time; to purchase within their reasonable financial means; to beware of excessive deficit spending and long-term, high-interest installment buying; to renounce luxuries which are inconsistent with the life of service and suffering; to set aside first their responsible giving to the church and its world ministries.*

A question which has agitated the conscience of many thoughtful Christians is the payment of taxes which may be used for purposes which they cannot endorse. The 1973 Brethren Annual Conference debated this issue at great length in consideration of a report by a study committee appointed a year earlier. This becomes a live issue when at least 60 percent of federal income taxes are used for war purposes and especially for a war that practically all Christians would decry as totally immoral and illegal.

Ina Ruth Addington, Brethren businesswoman, shares this opinion on paying taxes:

> *Yes, we should pay taxes. Ours is not a perfect, but it is the best government in the world; we should support it. Yet we should follow the dictates of our conscience and refuse to pay or pay under protest any taxes that support war or other actions contrary to Christian faith. This, too, is supportive. Much more so than paying the tax and then criticizing the government for levying it. We are obligated to let our voice be heard—to participate.*

Or this from Dorris Blough, homemaker:

> *This is one question we have been mulling over for a long time. If there was a close fellowship of courageous Brethren here, we probably would have stopped paying some of our taxes long ago. But it is an action which needs support of like-minded people. Our consciences are hurt because we are not doing it. We would like to refuse to pay taxes which support war in any way.*

Louise Bowman, secretary:

> *Yes, we should pay taxes. Brethren, or anyone, should protest specific taxation if the use of such taxes violates that person's integrity. If that person should refuse to pay such taxes, he should do so while accepting the consequences that may be imposed for nonpayment.*

Frank S. Carper, retired minister-banker:

> *Since Jesus paid tax, so far I could conscientiously pay my tax even though I deplore the use and waste of tax money.*

Erv and Joan Huston, teacher and nurse:

> *Yes, we should pay; yes, we should refuse and protest. We should refuse to pay voluntarily those taxes going for activities incongruent with Christian life-style, i.e. war and government subsidies to big business, or where government cuts back in programs caring for the "poor, the orphan, and the widow."*

Olden D. Mitchell, pastor:

> *Yes, many kinds of taxes, hidden and others. I feel we should refuse a tax specifically designated which violates our conscience, as was the telephone tax for the Southeast Asia war. Some other taxes I feel we should protest. But first we must make our concern heard in person and otherwise, as tax measures are being developed and passed, local, state, and nation.*

Melvin Slabaugh, retired merchant:

> *Yes, we should pay taxes. When tax money is used for destructive ends or exploitation, Christians have a responsibility to act as the nation's conscience through protest or refusal.*

The uneasy conscience of the Brethren is well reflected in these statements. Some would like to refuse payment of that portion of taxes which is used for war, but few have the courage to do it without assurance of full moral support from the church. But most agree that responsible citizenship requires that we "act as the nation's conscience" in active protest and by making our voices heard by those who levy and spend taxes. Some persons feel that one should seriously consider reducing one's income so that this issue would become academic.

This may not appeal to most people as a responsibile way to deal with the issue.

After their deaths, what responsibility do Christians have in the disposition of the money they may have accumulated? While to most people who are not particularly affluent, the question may not seem important, good stewardship calls for serious thought and wise planning. All adult persons should have a carefully drawn will, to make sure that their property, little or much, goes to those persons and causes they want to support. A Christian will is an element of good stewardship.

Earning, spending, saving, investing, giving, bequeathing our money are all aspects of good stewardship. Money can be put to many beautiful uses and bring blessing to all who use it. Or it can be a curse, a weapon, a trap, a disaster. A King Midas can destroy everything he touches, with his "golden touch." Or a David Livingstone can say, "I place no values on anything I possess, except in relation to the Kingdom of God."

Can the possession of wealth ever be consistent with the simple life? A recent article in a national magazine points out the interesting fact that most big Japanese businessmen live lives of frugality and simplicity, with much emphasis upon good home and family life, yet without ostentation and vulgar consumption.

Money can be beautiful and useful. It can buy food, clothing and medicine, dispel ignorance, serve as an instrument of *shalom*. It can give meaning to the energies that we expend in earning and getting. The Christian person and family will develop a lifestyle in which money is a blessed servant, never a master, in which money, much or little, is a sacred trust, used to further the purposes of the Kingdom of God.

Chapter 9

TRIUMPH OVER TECHNOLOGY

CHRISTIANS are called to affirm and give life in an age of swiftly advancing technology and unprecedented scientific discovery. This is a fact of our life from which we cannot hide or retreat. We may feel trapped by the machines which surround us, frustrated by computers which coldly refuse to admit their monumental mistakes, choked by the fumes of industry, shattered by the noise and relentless march of factories, trucks, and supersonic planes. But we need not despair. We need not be slaves of technology, nor need we reject it. For some persons, science and technology have become a religion.

Science is my shepherd, I shall not want;

He maketh me to lie down on foam rubber mattresses;

He leadeth me beside the eight-lane freeways.

He rejuvenateth my shattered psyche;

He leadeth me to the psychoanalyst's couch for peace of mind's sake.

Yea, though I walk in the valley of the shadow of the Iron Curtain, I will fear no communist; thy hydrogen bomb and thy Trident submarine, they comfort me.

Thou preparest a banquet before me in the presence of a billion starving people.

Thou anointest my head with hair restorers and eye shadow.

My beer glass foameth over.

Surely pleasure and affluence shall follow me
     all the days of my life,
And I shall dwell in Shangri-la forever.

Yes, that is cynical; yet it may serve to portray the utter dependence of so many people in our affluent society upon our technological society and our growth and consumer economy.

Our present concern for a simpler, uncluttered Christian life-style based upon seeking first the Kingdom of God and his *shalom* is not a nostalgic cry to return to the "good old days" of rural communities unsullied by factory smoke and automation. Can we and should we return to Thoreau's Walden Pond? To the security of the monastery? To the bucolic and robust rural church life at Baugo and Paradise Prairie? No. We can face our age with a Christian faith that God still reigns in our world and that we can have a life-style which does not reject or retreat from science and technology, or from our urban environment. This life-style can evaluate our culture and our technology, and refuses to be its dumb and apathetic slave and triumphantly lives in this world in simple and loving obedience to our Lord Jesus Christ. The challenge is to see what we can do as individuals and families to live simply, joyously, creatively and triumphantly in this kind of world, and what the church can do to help us, and to witness to God's *shalom* in this situation.

As Christians, we face a vast system based upon the conventional wisdom that bigger and faster always mean better; that all people inevitably benefit by expanding industry and accelerating Gross National Product; that science and technology are the panaceas for all human ills. But we must challenge these notions. We now see that the environmental costs of Western industrial development have been

tremendous. To continue at this rate will impover-
ish and swiftly destroy the life-support systems of
Earth. Also we now see that the benefits of industrialization are not equitably distributed. The rich
are steadily becoming richer; and even though the
poor have more in some places, the gap between
rich and poor is growing wider. We must measure
and evaluate science, technology, industry from the
theological conviction that God calls us to be prophetic witnesses for social justice and at the same
time responsible stewards of the Earth and its resources entrusted to us. Sometimes these two areas
of concern will conflict; sometimes they will con-
verge. The Christian always seeks to keep these
two concerns in balance, maintaining a world view,
and always seeks to take action in the light of the
needs of peoples in Africa, Bangladesh and China,
as well as in Iowa and Maryland. Appreciative of
the fruits of scientific discovery and technological
skills, the Christian will appreciate also the limits
of Earth's resources. As Norman Faramelli points
out:

> *In any issue we become involved in, we should
> ask: "What are the effects of present practices
> on the 'least of these my brethren'? Remember
> the biblical bias on behalf of the poor: "Seek
> justice, correct oppression, defend the father-
> less, plead for the widow" (Isaiah 1:18). That
> command for social justice must be at the
> heart of our environmental concerns.*

The issues we must face in the use or rejection of
the fruits of technology are complex. But in making
our decisions we can ask, "Does my use of this ob-
ject or machine contribute to the quality of my life
and that of my family? Will it cause me to consume
more than my share of resources? Will my use of it
deprive my sister or brother of sustenance and free-

dom? Will this free me for more service to my family and my community? Am I making this purchase
from the motivation of conspicuous consumption,
real need, or the enhancement of my life as a simple
follower of Jesus? Am I adding to the problems of
pollution, injustice, waste, and impoverishment of
Earth by buying and using this thing?"

Ken Shaffer comments on the use of the automobile:

> I often feel trapped by technology. For exam-
> ple, it is nearly impossible to function in our
> society without a car; and there are times
> when maintaining a car is pure frustration.
> Yet the frustration is rooted in the false as-
> sumption that I cannot live without a car.
> When I think life is impossible without a car,
> that car has begun to rule me, rather than
> serve me. Technology exists to better our lives,
> not determine our lives. We must learn to con-
> trol technology rather than ignore it or hide
> from it.

And Mary Baucher points up the dilemma many
Christian families face in the use of the automobile:

> I try to be involved with people and needs;
> time and distance require my use of a car.
> With three teenage boys all driving and all lik-
> ing activities that need cars or other engines
> (water skiing, snow skiing, etc.), I am torn be-
> tween ecology and allowing the boys to keep
> occupied with outdoor activities.

A different kind of problem is described by Virginia Fisher:

> When we were both gainfully employed, we
> both felt trapped by the distances we had to
> travel to our jobs. Time spent in commuting is
> so much time lost, in my book. But with the
> urbanization of society the way it is today,

people just cannot work out in the back pasture today and in the barn tomorrow.

We do not feel trapped by technology because it has given us many advantages—the daily paper which brings us the news at 4:30 each morning; listening to records of the greatest music ever composed played by the world's greatest artists; and the blessing of inexpensive books among other "gifts" of modern technology. I should mention our lovely grand piano at which so many people take music lessons.

A Christian life-style then does not reject technology or retreat from it. It baptizes its fruits and utilizes them in the service of the family and the neighbor. All technology, all gadgets, all scientific discoveries are our servants not our masters, in this way of life.

What can the church do to assist its members in developing such a life-style? In making a Christian witness in our technological society? We must first ask whether our present situation invites any specifically Christian response or responsibility. Are there actions or policies which the church can advocate and pursue which will have some hope of affecting the system for good?

Economist Barbara Ward, writing in Church of the Brethren *Messenger* (September 1973) says:

Whenever the Christian community has begun to renew itself, some of its saints and prophets have made a new effort to fight against the enormous temptations of wanting too much. As Rome collapsed, the monks went into the desert. As the barbarians took over Europe, St. Benedict set up his monasteries where all was simplicity, work, and prayer. As the first wave of high bourgeois prosperity broke over medieval Europe, St. Francis of Assisi made Lady Poverty his bride. At the beginnings of the commercial and industrial revolution in England, the Quakers rejected all luxury in dress and manner.

Not all Christians feel called to this total self-giving. But is there not a place for the renewal of the idea of a "third order" of Christian people who, voluntarily, cut back their consumption, abandon the dream of ever-rising prosperity, and begin seriously sharing their income with those who are in the greatest need? Can we be sure that such an example, joyfully made and explained, might not set social tides moving away from the greedy collective pressures which feed first inflation and then disaster?

Norman Faramelli, in *To Love or to Perish*, makes this statement of the role of the church:

In addition to traditional concerns for pastoral care, liturgy, et cetera, the role of the church in this decade should be threefold: (1) To offer a systematic and prophetic critique of technological society; (2) To build new visions of what alternative futures we may be able to work for and to shape criteria for their selection; and (3) To provide clues and means for translating visions into social realities, or getting us from "here" to "there."

Here are some suggestions from Brethren on what we might do.

Study what a simple life means in the seventies. Study and act more on what we are doing to our environment. Push for disarmament. Elect better officials. Run for office ourselves. Build koinonia fellowships among lots of different peoples—more youth groups meeting together—more adults meeting with youth to explore what an integrated life-style means in our age. We need to live more in balance with nature.—Virginia Fisher

Strong emphasis on the home, and searching the Scriptures. The church should emphasize conservation, economy, the many free things that are fun to do. Teach honesty, good character, concern for others.—Wayne Spangler, educator

Continually promote Christian stewardship with emphasis on the simple life as the highest ideal of stewardship. Develop models of simple living as examples to challenge the whole denomination.—Franklin K. Cassel, physician

If simple life is an end in itself, forget it! If it is an outgrowth of Christian discipleship, then deepening commitment and obedience would be the first steps. Encourage discussions, help us to realize there is a realistic, desirable option, arrived at through study of the New Testament. To know a person who lives simply encourages me more than any other thing, a person's example and sharing of his faith.—Mary Baucher, homemaker

Educate! People must learn to distinguish between their own needs and the needs the advertisers create for them. People must learn that personal satisfaction comes from fellowship with others rather than gratifications of their every desire. People must learn how to live the life-style presented in the New Testament. Furthermore, since part of education is experience, they must begin to experience the simple life, not as a code of laws, but as life in harmony with God's creation.—Ken Shaffer

One suggestion for vital experimentation which

might well provide a model for other areas to study
is made by Jason Bauserman:

> *I have talked informally to several people
> about forming a Brethren community. If a
> farm were willed to the church, that would be
> an ideal situation for experiment. Those inter-
> ested in living a simple life could come, learn,
> build, and help others do the same. I know of
> many young people in the church today who
> would love to be a part of this. I am positive
> this would be of real significance to many of
> our searching youth. This would be a viable
> ministry that would pay dividends—if it was
> Christ-centered. I would like to see it tried.*

Almost all of those I interviewed in preparing this
book expressed deep concern that we make a strong
effort to develop a life-style that is simple in the
biblical sense of being Christ-centered, emphasizing
the spiritual over the material.

As I see it, such a life-style should be based upon
Matthew 6:33—seek first the Kingdom of God and
his justice. It would be a life-style which does not
look backward with nostalgia, but that uses the insights gained by our ancestors in building a viable,
creative life-style now. It affirms strongly the
Christian view of creation and sees persons as "tenants of the Almighty." We are to be concerned for
the conservation and the renewal of Earth. We are
to be concerned for the whole human family affirming our kinship with all the children of God, responsible for their well-being. We are to confront
the vast ecological and social problems of our time
not by a frightened retreat from the world, or by
giving up our dreams of "Our Father's World" as
impractical or utopian. The course of human history has often been changed by small groups who
have dreamed a great dream and sought to com-

mend it to the world in courageous witness and demonstration.

The Brethren have always found good reasons for living simply, sometimes through economic and social pressures. Now the necessities are compelling for nearly everyone. It is now a matter of life and breath—and death—for us and for all people.

T. Wayne Rieman suggests:

Perhaps this is our life task: to focus diffused goodwill. To focus high thoughts of God and Jesus on the world's problems. To raise to the point of burning zeal the desire to alleviate the suffering, exploitation, and injustices of our Earth. To invent new life-styles appropriate to the love of neighbor in a world of limited resources. To explore ways of subverting the affluent world which cares so little for Christ's favorite people—the poor. To teach others how to swim against the stream of uncaring affluence, wastage of the resources of our good Earth, and the ruthless exploitation of people. Are not these the incarnation of the Good News in our era?

Our little efforts will not feed the hungry, clothe the naked, right the economic wrongs of the world. No. Let's not be pretentious. But they are beginnings—starting points. A recent cover statement of Christianity and Crisis *put it together, "Not to make an effort would be to die in life, and that is what I lament in others."*

Set your mind on God's Kingdom and his justice before everything else, and all the rest will come to you as well. Purity of heart, simplicity of life, is to will this one thing.

BIBLIOGRAPHY

BOOKS

Arnold, Eberhard, *The Early Christians*. Rifton, New York: The Plough Publishing House, 1970, $10.00.

———*Why We Live in Community*. Rifton, New York: The Plough Publishing House, 1967, $.30.

Arnold, Emmy, *Torches Together*. Rifton, New York: The Plough Publishing House, 1971, $4.95.

Baker, May Allread, *The Gift of the Year*. Elgin: The Brethren Press, 1964, $2.90.

Bailey, Liberty Hyde, *The Holy Earth*. New York: Gordon Press, $11.75.

Campbell, Rex R. and Jerry L. Wade, *Society and Environment: The Coming Collision*. Boston: Allyn and Bacon, 1972, $4.95.

Carr, Jo and Imogene Sorley, *The Intentional Family*. Nashville: Abingdon Press, 1971, $3.50.

Carothers, J. Edward, Margaret Mead, Daniel J. McCracken, and Roger Shinn, eds., *To Live or To Perish*. New York: Friendship Press, 1972, $4.95.

Carson, Rachel, *Silent Spring*. New York: Houghton Mifflin Co., 1962, $6.95, pap. $2.95.

Christman, R. F. et al, *The Natural Environment: Wastes and Control*, Pacific Palisades: Goodyear Publishing Co., 1973, $7.95.

Day, Dorothy, *Loaves and Fishes*. New York: Curtis Books Inc., 1972, $1.25.

Drucker, Peter F., *The Age of Discontinuity*. New York: Harper and Row, 1968, $7.95.

Durnbaugh, Donald F., *The Believers' Church*. New York: The MacMillan Co., 1968, $7.95.

———*European Origins of the Brethren*. Elgin: The Brethren Press, 1958, $5.95.

———ed., *The Church of the Brethren, Past and Present*. Elgin: The Brethren Press, 1971, $3.95.

Ehrlich, Paul, *The Population Bomb*. New York: Ballantine Books, Inc., 1971, $.95.

——and Richard Harriman, *How To Be a Survivor*. New
York: Ballantine Books, Inc., 1971, $5.95, pap. $1.25.

Elder, Frederick, *Crisis in Eden: A Religious Study of Man
and Environment*. Nashville: Abingdon Press, 1970,
$3.95.

Eller, Vernard, *The Mad Morality*. Nashville: Abingdon
Press, 1970, $2.79.

——*The Simple Life: The Christian Stance Toward Possessions*. Grand Rapids: William B. Eerdmans Publishing Co., 1973, $2.25.

Ellul, Jacques, *The Technological Society*. New York: Random House, Inc., $2.45.

Ford, Leighton, *One Way to Change the World*. New York:
Harper and Row, 1970, $3.95.

Galbraith, John Kenneth, *The Affluent Society*. New York.
Houghton Mifflin Co., 1971, $2.95.

Gibbons, Euell, *Stalking the Wild Asparagus*. New York:
David McKay, Field Guide Edition, 1970, $7.95, pap.
$2.95.

Gingerich, Melvin, *Mennonite Attire Through Four Centuries*. Breinigsville, Pa.: The Pennsylvania German
Society, 1970.

Gish, Arthur G., *Beyond the Rat Race*. New Canaan, Ct.:
Keats Publishing, Inc., 1973, $1.45.

Graham, Frank Jr., *Since Silent Spring*. New York: Faw-
cett World Library, 1970, $.95.

Heis, Richard L. and Noel F. McInnis, eds., *Can Man Care
For the Earth?* Nashville: Abingdon Press, 1971,
$1.95.

Higbee, Edward, *A Question of Priorities: New Strategies
for Our Urbanized World*. New York: William Mor-
row Company, Inc., 1970, $2.25.

Kagawa, Toyohiko, *Brotherhood Economics*. New York:
Harper and Brothers, 1936, O.P.

Kelly, Thomas R., *A Testament of Devotion*. New York:
Harper and Brothers, 1941, $3.95.

Klotz, John W., Ecology Crisis: *God's Creation and Man's
Pollution*. St. Louis: Concordia Publishing House,
1971, $2.75.

Leopold, Aldo, *A Sand County Almanac*. New York: Oxford University Press, 1966, $7.50.

Mallott, Floyd E., *Is Life Worth Living?* New Lebanon,
Ohio: Ruth B. Mallott, 1972, $4.25.

Metzler, Burton, *Light From a Hillside*. Elgin: The Brethren Press, 1968, $1.95.

Miller, Dewitt L. and Mary, *If Two Are to Become One*. Elgin: The Brethren Press, 1960, $1.25.

Moomaw, Ira W., *The Challenge of Hunger*. New York: Frederick A. Praeger, 1966, $5.95.

————*Crusade Against Hunger*. New York: Harper and Row, 1966, $3.95.

————*To Hunger No More*. New York: Friendship Press, 1963, $1.95.

Packard, Vance, *The Hidden Persuaders*. New York: Pocket Books, $.95.

Raper, Arthur, *Tenants of the Almighty*. New York: Arno Press, 1971, $23.00.

Rienow, Robert and Leona, *Moment in the Sun*. New York: Ballantine Books, Inc., 1969, $.95.

Rupel, Esther Fern, "An Investigation of the Origin Significance, and Demise of the Prescribed Dress Worn by Members of the Church of the Brethren." Unpublished Ph.D. dissertation, University of Minnesota Graduate School, 1971.

Russell, Ota Lee, *Jackknife Summer*. Elgin: The Brethren Press, 1958, $2.25.

Thoreau, Henry David, *Walden*. New York: Houghton Mifflin Co., $1.10.

Thomas À Kempis, *The Imitation of Christ*. Baltimore: Penguin Books, $1.45.

Toffler, Alvin, *Future Shock*. New York: Random House, 1970, $8.95.

Trueblood, Elton, *The New Man For Our Time*. New York: Harper and Row, 1970, $2.95.

Ward, Barbara, *Rich Nations and Poor Nations*. New York: W.W. Norton and Company, Inc., 1962, $1.25.

White, Roy, *Venturing South*. Elgin: The Brethren Press, 1958, $3.00.

Williams, Cecil B., *Paradise Prairie*. New York: The John Day Co., 1953, O.P.

Yoder, Glee, *Take It From Here*. Valley Forge, Pa.: Judson Press, 1973, $2.50.

MAGAZINES

Messenger, Church of the Brethren, Elgin, Ill.

National Geographic, National Geographic Society, Washington, D.C.

National Wildlife

Saturday Review/World, Saturday Review/World Inc., New York.

FOR FURTHER READING

The Simple Life. Vernard Eller. $2.25
An exploration of the impact of New Testament teachings regarding the simple life—the attitude toward material possessions recommended and practiced by Jesus.

Beyond the Rat Race. Arthur Gish. $1.45
Presents simplicity as a life-style to free man from the pressures of competing in a complex society.

Messenger. Official magazine for the Church of the Brethren.
Interprets trends and current happenings within the Church. Proclaims the gospel through Biblical studies, faith statements, and theological probes. Builds continuity with the past and with the future. Messenger for such a time as this. Monthly. $5.00 yearly subscription.

Brethren Life and Thought
A quarterly journal with "life and thought" styles of the Church of the Brethren. It is filled with articles on how the once visible "plain people" are expressing their simple living in today's world. $6.00 yearly subscription.

The Brethren Press, 1451 Dundee Ave., Elgin, Ill. 60120